THE ELEMENT GUIDE

ANOREXIA & BULIMIA

Julia Buckroyd is a psychotherapist and counsellor who has spent many years working with people needing help with both anorexia and bulimia. She spent five years as the Student Counsellor at London Contemporary Dance School. She is now Principal Lecturer in Counselling at the University of Hertfordshire, England. She continues to maintain a private practice and to lecture and run workshops. She is also the author of *Eating Your Heart Out* (Optima).

• THE ELEMENT GUIDE •

ANOREXIA & BULIMIA

Your Questions Answered

Julia Buckroyd

ELEMENT

Shaftesbury, Dorset • Rockport, Massachusetts
Brisbane, Queensland

Text © Julia Buckroyd 1996

First published in Great Britain in 1996 by
Element Books Limited
Shaftesbury, Dorset SP7 8BP

Published in the USA in 1996 by
Element Books, Inc.
PO Box 830, Rockport, MA 01966

Published in Australia in 1996 by
Element Books Limited
for Jacaranda Wiley Limited
33 Park Road, Milton, Brisbane 4064

Reprinted May 1996

Cover design by Max Fairbrother
Page design by Roger Lightfoot
Typeset by Footnote Graphics, Warminster, Wiltshire
Printed and bound in Great Britain by Biddles Ltd,
Guildford & King's Lynn

British Library Cataloguing in Publication
data available

Library of Congress Cataloging in Publication
data available

ISBN 1-85230-776-5

Note from the Publisher
Any information given in any book in *The Element Guide* series is not
intended to be taken as a replacement for medical advice. Any person
with a condition requiring medical attention should consult a qualified
medical practitioner or suitable therapist.

Contents

for Karin

Preface

This book owes much to my clients, anorexic and bulimic, from whom I have learned most of what I know. I would like to thank them for allowing me to enter their private worlds and to come to understand with them the meanings and purposes of the ways they use food.

My thanks are also due to those colleagues with whom I have shared my thoughts in lectures, workshops and informal discussions and who have stimulated me to continuing reflection and exploration.

My students on the counselling courses at the University of Hertfordshire in England have provided me with the opportunity to try out theories and ideas and have helped me clarify my thinking. I would particularly like to thank Sheila O'Donnell for permission to use her concept of 'Planet Anorexia'.

I am grateful to Wendy Dobbs, with whom I worked at Vector and with whom some of the 'help yourself' strategies were evolved.

I am particularly indebted to Karin Thulin, whose interest in psychosomatic illness has often enlightened my work on eating disorders and who has been a continuing source of support and encouragement, both personally and professionally.

Throughout the book I have used 'she' to refer to the person with an eating disorder because 'he or she' is unbearably clumsy. However there are men who are anorexic or bulimic; I hope that they will be able to locate themselves in the pronouns of the opposite gender.

I am not very happy about the use of the words 'anorexic' and 'bulimic' as nouns; it is hard to be defined by one's psychological condition. I am afraid, however, that I have not been able to avoid it entirely. I can only say in my defence that for some years now my main preoccupation has been to persuade the person with an eating disorder that she is more than her affliction.

Introduction

This book has been written primarily as a guide for people suffering from anorexia or bulimia and for their families and friends. It may also be useful as an overview of the subject for some health professionals.

There has been huge amount of publicity given to these conditions in recent years, so that most of us at least know of their existence and that anorexics starve themselves whereas bulimics binge and vomit. Many people know little more than that. Certainly it is not widely understood that anorexia and bulimia are not just to do with food use but are part of an emotional system that affects every aspect of the sufferer's life. This book therefore begins with a description of the behaviour of someone who is anorexic or bulimic and the physical and psychological effects of that behaviour. People with these disorders are often assumed to be able to give them up if only they tried a little; I have therefore attempted to show how strong the grip of anorexia and bulimia can be and how compulsive the urge to starve or binge and vomit can become

Even quite wide reporting of anorexia in the media generally fails to provide any understanding of *why* a person should find it necessary to behave in such strange and self-destructive ways, yet there has been extensive writing on the subject, especially in the past 15 years. In the second section of the book I therefore give an outline of the two main lines of thinking. Nowadays most researchers agree that anorexia and bulimia have something to do both with the individual's personal history and family background and with the cultural and societal pressures to which women in westernized industrial countries are subjected. Anorexia and bulimia will therefore have a meaning and purpose in the life of the individual, but that meaning will be reinforced by wider cultural influences.

It may seem strange to think of anorexia and bulimia as having meaning and purpose, and there are some clinicians who regard them simply as bad habits which sufferers should be forced to give up. The fact that these conditions affect only women, in a highly specific cultural setting, however, strongly suggests that they are to do with women's sense of themselves and are responses to a given set of circumstances. It is extremely worrying that these conditions are so common, but in my view that reflects widespread distress among women about the way their lives have to be lived. The long-term answers lie in deeper social changes; the short-term answers must include a response to the distress of the individual.

The question of cure then is complex. In the third section of this book I provide some ways in which sufferers can help themselves and describe the different kinds of treatment that are available from professionals. Gradually a consensus is emerging among clinicians that getting better has to take place on several fronts at the same time. The sufferer must find her way back to a normal pattern of eating, and in order to do this she will need a lot of practical help and support. She must also start to undo the habits of thought about food and about size, weight and shape that keep her prisoner. Thirdly, she must start to understand why she has *needed* her illness and what function it has had for her. These three aspects of recovery – behavioural, cognitive and therapeutic – all need to be addressed if the sufferer is not only to recover from her eating disorder but also develop as a person to the point where she does not need it any more.

Over the past 20 years, treatment programmes have often focused on one of these aspects to the exclusion of others. Anorexics and bulimics frequently complain that the response they find most often is behavioural: doctors and those around them are desperate to change the eating behaviour, but seem to show little understanding of its nature or purpose. In recent years this single focus has begun to change. As the following pages will show, anyone looking for help, or embarking on helping themselves or someone else, should bear in mind the need to attend to all three aspects.

Over the years in which I have been working with people with eating disorders I have very often encountered despair in both sufferers and their families, about whether they can find help and whether it is possible ever to recover from anorexia and bulimia. Underneath those questions I hear a cry of anguish about whether the sufferer can possibly find a more satisfying way to live her life. I hope this book can contribute to understanding and recovery, and that it will help sufferers and those who love them embark together on the process of change and growth.

SECTION ONE

What are Anorexia and Bulimia?

CHAPTER 1

What is Anorexia?

Everyone else in my class was going on a diet, so I did too, except that they all stopped and I didn't. To start with I was pleased. I felt proud that I had more will-power than they did, but in the end it was awful because I couldn't stop dieting. They had all lost a few pounds so that they could get into a size smaller dress, but I just went on and on. In the end I got so I was frightened to eat anything. In one part of my head I knew that I had to eat and that I needed to eat, but in another I thought I was fat and that if I ate anything it would make me even fatter. That was when I was less than 6 stones [84lb/38kg].

What is anorexia? How do you know you have got it? What does it do to you? In this chapter I will try and define anorexia and describe how it affects not only eating behaviour and weight but also other parts of a sufferer's life.

THE CLINICAL DESCRIPTION

Anorexia has been known and recognized by doctors for at least 300 years. Initially the characteristic that was most described was the striking weight loss and emaciation resulting from a failure to eat. There are, however, a number of organic illnesses that result in loss of appetite and consequent weight loss, and so from the late 19th century doctors tried to describe more exactly what anorexia was and began to exclude organic causes and to identify it as a psychological illness.

This process of definition has continued until the present day, with continuing attempts to clarify whether there might be any organic malfunction which has a part to play in the illness. At this point, however, the overwhelming evidence seems to indicate that anorexia is, in the words of the doctors, a 'psychiatric disorder' and has no organic, metabolic or genetic cause.

These are frightening words, 'psychiatric disorder', but we can perhaps make them less intimidating by considering in more detail what they mean in the case of anorexia.

The definition of anorexia that has been most widely used in recent years is one developed by the American Psychiatric Association and published in 1987:

Diagnostic criteria for anorexia nervosa

1 Refusal to maintain body weight over a minimal normal weight for age and height, eg weight loss leading to maintenance of body weight 15 per cent below that expected; or failure to make expected weight gain during period of growth, leading to body weight 15 per cent below that expected
2 Intense fear of gaining weight or becoming fat, even though underweight
3 Disturbance in body image, eg the person claims to 'feel fat' even when emaciated or believes one area of the body to be 'too fat' even when obviously underweight
4 In females, absence of at least three consecutive menstrual cycles when otherwise expected to occur

(DSM-III-R, American Psychiatric Association, 1987)

To this basic outline can be added a series of other characteristics which may accompany the most central features of anorexia:

- hair loss
- growth of lanugo – fine hair growing all over the body, including on the face
- lowered body temperature and heart rate
- low blood pressure
- feeling cold
- poor circulation
- dry skin
- brittle nails

- insomnia
- excessive exercising directed to weight loss
- obsessional focus on food and calories
- loneliness, social isolation, withdrawn behaviour
- loss of the ability to concentrate on anything else
- low self-esteem
- self-hatred

SUB-CLINICAL ANOREXIA

The clinical descriptions given above have been devised by doctors working with anorexics who are sufficiently ill to have been referred to them in hospitals. They were developed for the benefit of American medical insurance companies who wanted a strict definition of the illnesses they were paying out for, and they have been widely used by doctors who like clear and unequivocal diagnoses.

These criteria, however, describe only the more advanced stages of the illness. What about those many individuals whose symptoms are not as serious as some of those described above? Are they anorexic or not? What about the girl who has lost a stone (14lb/6.5kg) in weight over the past 6 months, finds excuses not to eat with her family, announces that she has become a vegetarian and refuses to eat 'fat' in any form? Is she anorexic? What about the girl who has been losing weight gradually over a year, does not want to socialize because she says she feels too fat and ugly and has regular but slight periods. Is she anorexic? What about the 15-year-old girl who is 5ft 6in (1.7m) tall and a size 8, whose periods have not started, who cuts the fat off meat, will not have butter on her bread, says she is 'too fat' and weighs herself several times a day? Is she anorexic?

I think it is certain that there are many young women who suffer from a mild degree of anorexia and who never come to the attention of a doctor, or who have been developing anorexia for a long time before they do. They manifest many of the characteristics of the illness to a moderate degree, suffer a good deal from it and would benefit from some help to get over it. And just as it is easier to deal with physical illness sooner rather than later, so it is easier to help someone with anorexia when they have an early form of the illness rather than when the obsessions and phobias have become a way of life.

INCIDENCE OF ANOREXIA

It is extremely difficult to know how many people develop anorexia. There is probably a good deal of under-reporting, especially of milder forms of the condition. A conservative figure puts the incidence at about 1 per cent of the female population between the ages of 15 and 30, but other estimates for particular groups, eg dancers, are much higher. The incidence has increased steadily in the developed world in the years since the Second World War and looks set to continue to rise. There are also reports of an increasing incidence in children. Estimates of the incidence in young men vary between one in ten and one in 20 reported cases, but it seems that with men, too, the incidence is increasing.

Anorexia used to be thought of as something that was restricted to the white middle classes, but researchers today say that they are seeing anorexics from all classes and ethnic groups. It is possible, however, that this change is merely the result of greater awareness of the illness and consequently wider reporting of it.

Estimates of mortality rates vary, but some figures suggest that between 6 and 10 per cent of sufferers die as a result of anorexia.

EATING PATTERNS IN ANOREXICS

Anorexia usually develops over a period of time, during which the sufferer changes her eating patterns from normal (or somewhere near normal) to a very restricted diet. This process can take months or years. It often seems to start with a young woman going on a diet. There is nothing unusual in this, but what is different for the person who may develop anorexia is that it is not as difficult for her as it is for most people. She comes to enjoy the feelings of hunger and seems to be able to discipline herself in a way that *is* very unusual; most people who go on diets have great difficulty keeping to them and do not enjoy the process at all. Then, as though she has discovered a talent in herself, the developing anorexic continues to diet even when she has reached her desired weight or the original period for dieting is finished. This again is unusual; most dieters are relieved to finish a diet and promptly return to their former patterns of eating.

Anorexia does not always begin in this way. Sometimes it starts with cutting out food that is considered to be fattening. For example, a teenage girl might start by not eating butter, oil or fat of any kind. What begins with cutting off all visible fat on meat may progress to refusing to eat any fried food, then to not putting any butter or margarine on sandwiches, to avoiding biscuits or cake because they have fat in them, to refusing to eat meat because it is 'fatty', to using only skimmed milk, to a truly panic reaction to eating food prepared by someone else in case it has fat in it.

Typically, this pattern then extends to other food, such as sugar. In time the budding anorexic can end up eating a diet that is nutritionally very unsound. Many anorexics have, for example, become vegetarians or vegans on the way to developing anorexia, and while it is perfectly possible to eat a nutritionally sound vegetarian or vegan diet, these people interpret vegetarianism as eating mostly fruit and vegetables. Nutritional needs for fat, protein and carbohydrate are not met.

Others move from cutting out specific food to eating very little at all of any kind. What little they do eat can be nutritionally very inadequate – for example a chocolate bar and black coffee to get them through the day. Others will pride themselves on eating only what is pure and good, but will attempt to survive on apples and black tea.

Some anorexics find food that they discover is 'non-fattening', like salad, vegetables, apples or crispbread, and will allow themselves to eat large quantities of such food. These foods will be thought of as good, while the vast majority of food is seen as bad. An anorexic who is thoroughly absorbed in her restricted way of eating can become exceedingly distressed if required to eat even small quantities of these 'bad' foods. She has become food-phobic and has as much terror and panic at the prospect of eating a roast dinner as a claustrophobic has at the thought of going to a party in a crowded room.

Whatever the process, the anorexic arrives at a point where what she takes in is inadequate to maintain her ordinary expected weight. The number of calories she absorbs is simply not enough. What began as a restriction of intake has become progressive starvation; there is no end or stopping place. What started as control has gone out of control.

All of this is done in the name of becoming less fat, even though to the ordinary eye the sufferer is anything but fat. It is also done at the price of denying hunger. For the person who feels the compulsive need to starve, hunger is a dreadful temptation rather than the friendly reminder from her body of the need to eat. That message from her body will be so thoroughly and effectively subdued and transformed that she will be able to say – and believe – that she is not hungry and does not feel hungry.

ANOREXIC EATING BEHAVIOUR

It is impossible to feel as anxious about getting fat and as frightened of food as an anorexic does and still be able to continue to eat with other people in a normal way. The phobias of anorexia are so difficult to manage that the anorexic will gradually isolate herself from other people so that she can continue with her anorexic behaviour. This does not necessarily happen all at once or very quickly.

Amanda had been accustomed to eating an evening meal with her parents and two brothers. For some months she had been eating less and less, despite the efforts of her parents to encourage her to eat more and the comments of her brothers that she was getting skinny and anorexic. At the beginning of the new school year she told her mother that she was going to do her homework at her friend's house and so would be home later. To her mother's enquiries about when she would eat, she replied that she would eat at her friend's house. Eventually her continuing weight loss made her mother make further enquiries, only to discover that for several weeks Amanda had not eaten an evening meal of any kind.

It is this kind of behaviour that leads to anorexics being labelled deceitful, but it is important to remember that food and eating have become sources of huge anxiety. Why that may be so will be discussed later.

What is often hard for families to bear is that frequently an anorexic woman will want to prepare food but will refuse to eat it herself and insist that it is eaten by others.

Caroline had taught herself to make French pastries and would spend hours creating the most amazing and delicious concoctions, glazed and decorated and stuffed with cream. She liked to present these to her family for dessert on Sundays, but would refuse to eat a mouthful herself saying that she was 'stuffed' and that in any case she had been eating while she made them. Her unhappy family would sit eating the pastries without being able to enjoy them while Caroline looked on and asked at intervals whether they were good.

There are many other ways in which an anorexic will attempt to hide her inadequate diet from those around her who have noticed her weight loss and are urging her to eat. She may, for example, take food, saying that she is going to eat it later but in fact giving it to others or throwing it away. Many a packed lunch has been disposed of like this. Sometimes food is hidden in a napkin or a pocket instead of being eaten and then later thrown away.

It fairly soon becomes impossible for a person who is becoming anorexic to conduct a normal social life, however, because so many social occasions are built round eating and drinking. Initially a young person may try and avoid eating or drinking, for instance by going to the pub but drinking mineral water, or going out for a pizza but eating only salad, or going round to a friend's house and claiming to have eaten already. However, these halfway stages tend to give way to eating secretly and alone.

> Betsy lived in a student hall of residence where she could use a cafeteria or cook for herself. Most of her fellow students arranged to eat together in groups but Betsy never ate in the cafeteria or the communal kitchen; she ate secretly, alone in her room.

As the illness continues the sufferer may well start to observe very precise rituals in relation to food, for instance eating exactly the same things at the same times each day. If she exceeds her self-imposed ration then she may punish herself later in the day by going without food altogether because she has been 'greedy'. If it is impossible to eat at the appointed time she may become agitated and anxious. She may cut everything up very small and very precisely, or chew every mouthful a fixed number of times. There may be a special plate or cup that she has to use. And if for any reason these conditions cannot be satisfied then she will not eat at all.

One way or another, by degrees, the anorexic person will become increasingly preoccupied with food, weight, shape and size, and less and less available for ordinary life. She will tend to withdraw progressively from social interaction and spend large amounts of time on her own. She will be thinking all day long about how much she has eaten, how much she will eat, how she can limit her intake further, and so on. This preoccupation with food is not unusual for someone who is starving; what is strange is that the anorexic behaves like someone who is starving while food is all around her. The stress and conflict created by her biological need to eat and her psychological fear of doing so uses up most of her time and energy.

ANOREXIA AND THE COMPULSION TO EXERCISE

This restriction of food and its effects are bad enough, but the anorexic obsession tends to extend to other areas of life as well. Although what observers notice is the preoccupation with food, that is only part of the anorexic's concern with weight and size. Because she believes she is fat and wants to be thin, she will often put herself on an exercise regime which she says is to keep her fit, but which in fact is intended to 'burn fat'.

> Dawn's PE teacher had recommended that the girls in her class try and improve their fitness by running. She recommended 2 miles (3.25km) three times a week. As Dawn became more and more anorexic she increased this programme until she was running 2 miles every day and then increased the distance from 2 to 4 and eventually to 6 miles a day. That meant she was running 42 miles (67km) a week – about a marathon and a half. Not surprisingly she lost weight, but not content with her programme she added a regime of strenuous exercises. It became an increasingly distressing sight for her family to see her forcing herself, thin and weak though she was, to 'keep fit'.

It is extremely bizarre to find anorexics who are so undernourished that their muscles have wasted away protesting that they must be allowed to undertake vigorous exercise. Again it is hard for those around them to understand that their exercising is born of fear and of compulsion. It can all too easily seem like wilful defiance, especially when the anorexic exercises secretly, for example in the middle of the night.

> Eileen's father woke up in the early hours of the morning to

hear strange scuffling noises. When he went to investigate he
discovered Eileen doing press-ups beside her bed.

BEING IN CONTROL

However central the ideas of weight, shape and size are,
there is a concept even more powerful for the anorexic and
that is the idea of control. This control is first of all exerted
over her food intake and her size, but in many anorexics it
extends to other areas of life.

Sleep is one area where anorexics often exercise control
by limiting what they allow themselves. Even though a
young woman may have exhausted herself by exercising
on an inadequate diet, she may force herself to do without
adequate sleep. Anorexics are full of self-criticism so she
will probably be telling herself that if she sleeps more than
a minimum number of hours, she is lazy, in very much the
same way that she will call herself greedy if she gives in to
her body's need for food.

It may also be easier for anorexics to do without enough
sleep because their starvation often makes them physically
restless. There is a theory based on an analogy with ani-
mal behaviour that we are built in such a way that if we
are starving our bodies will create a rather frantic energy
so that we can search for food. Certainly many anorexics
seem to have more energy than might be expected, given
their very limited food intake. Eventually, however, pro-
longed starvation brings weakness and exhaustion which
even an anorexic cannot overcome.

In a similar way a person suffering from anorexia may
deprive herself of adequate clothing, even though she is
likely to feel the cold more acutely than those who are
insulated with a layer of fat and whose circulation func-
tions well.

Fiona worked in a garden centre and was outside in all
weathers. To the amazement and horror of her employer she
never wore more than jeans and a T-shirt. When questioned

about it she would say that she was used to the cold and besides, working kept her warm. This was not very convincing when it was plain that her hands were blue with cold.

Some anorexics know that the body uses more energy to keep warm if it is not adequately clothed and add that to the number of ways in which they can lose weight. Others talk about not needing or not deserving to be warm. It can often sound as though an anorexic is punishing herself for having a body that needs to keep warm, or indeed has any needs at all.

This self-deprivation often extends also to money. Some anorexics can be generous with others, for example buying presents, but operate a ruthlessly parsimonious regime for themselves.

Gillian refusued to buy herself some sticking plasters to put on her blistered heel, saying that she did not need them, although the blood had come through her sock and her heel was obviously painful.

Hilda bought all her clothes from jumble sales and charity shops. She said she could not see the point of buying new clothes when second-hand ones were just as good.

Anorexics can even tightly restrict their use of time they spend on their own pleasures.

Ian was keen on computers, but he limited himself to half an hour a day at the screen. He felt it was self-indulgent to spend more time doing something he liked and that was just for him.

Jennifer would never spend more than a rigidly timed ten minutes in the bath. Any more than that and she felt 'selfish'.

PUTTING LIFE ON HOLD

It will be obvious by now that what begins as food restriction in anorexia has the potential to develop into a way of life that affects the whole of the sufferer's existence and leaves little room for anything else. Enormous amounts of time and energy can be spent planning and fantasizing about the details of day-to-day life. Moreover, this system is secret and must be kept like that. The secrecy also takes much effort and planning and further separates the anorexic from her peers and her family. It can be as though she is living on a different planet – Planet Anorexia.

It is impossible for a young woman living on Planet Anorexia to mature or develop as she should according to her age. Most researchers now feel that a sufferer is only as old as the age she was when the anorexia first developed, even though chronologically she may be much older. Anorexia stunts and inhibits growth and development in every part of the sufferer's life. It is probably designed to do exactly that; it is a way of saying, 'Stop the world, I want to get off!'

Physical effects

Anorexia slows or prevents growth and halts pubertal development. There are researchers who think that the entire purpose of anorexia may be to reverse pubertal development and to return the body to a pre-pubertal state; that anorexia is a refusal to go through the process of developing and growing up. Although most researchers do not believe anorexia can be explained in this way in all cases, it is certainly true that physically that is its effect.

When anorexia begins before a girl has reached puberty, she will not go through the expected pubertal changes. A child of 11 who becomes seriously anorexic will not grow in height and will not undergo the other skeletal changes in body shape that puberty brings about, so her pelvis will remain narrow and untilted, like a child's. Her hair and skin will remain those of a child. She will not develop the breasts, hips and buttocks characteristic of a woman. Because her hormones remain those of a child, menstruation will not be established and she will not experience the awakening of sexual interest which the hormonal changes of puberty create. Physically she will remain a child.

Fortunately anorexia at this early age is not very common, although research suggests that it is becoming more so, but there are anorexics in their teens and twenties who look like children because of the stunting of physical development that the condition has caused.

When anorexia begins after pubertal development has got under way, these changes will be partly reversed, although the changes to the skeleton are fortunately not reversible. However the fat deposits on breasts, hips, abdomen, buttocks and thighs can all be removed by starvation, and menstruation and sexual awareness can be reversed.

When an anorexic recovers, most aspects of the process of physical development can be resumed and a normal body shape will return. Skeletal changes, however, will probably not take place if they have not done so before the onset of anorexia. Although menstruation will usually start or be resumed spontaneously, this does not always happen and when it does, it frequently takes a considerable time, even after normal weight has been achieved. There is some evidence that former anorexics can find it difficult to resume normal ovulation and can have problems in conceiving naturally.

It is known that failure to menstruate means that oestrogen levels are low and that as a result bone density development is permanently affected. Although bone density will improve when oestrogen levels rise again, the former anorexic will not catch up on the development she has missed and will therefore be at risk of osteoporosis in later life.

Intellectual effects

Although anorexics often study or work extremely hard, even obsessively, their work suffers because their emotional life and creative capacities are so limited by their illness.

> Marlene was a dance student who managed very well in her training, despite her developing anorexia, so long as all that was required of her was to perform the steps exactly as she had been taught. When she was asked to interpret the movement and put something of herself into it, she found it impossible. Then when she was asked to choreograph short pieces herself, she covered her paralysis with anger, saying that it was ridiculous to ask students to choreograph when it was obvious that the great choreographers had provided ballets that were much more worthwhile.

In the same way students suffering from anorexia can come to grief when they are asked for a personal response to what they are reading. So much effort has been invested in having no needs or feelings of their own that they do not know what they feel about what they are reading, although they will often know a great deal about what everybody else has felt and said about it.

In other words, a person with anorexia finds it entirely possible to work hard at reproducing information and will often do it brilliantly. This hard work will pay off as long as that is all that is required of her. However as time goes on, especially after she gets to the age of 16 or so, she will increasingly be asked for her own opinions, ideas and responses and find it more difficult to succeed. The fact is that she has emptied herself of herself, and so long as she is anorexic she has nothing much to give.

Social effects

As we have already seen, the anorexic is likely to have withdrawn into isolation. Self-starvation demands enormous emotional energy and concentration, and leaves little room for anything or anyone else. Sexually she is prepubertal and often as innocent of sexual attraction as a child.

However it is not just that the anorexic girl has withdrawn from ordinary social interchange; her behaviour means that her social development has become stuck at whatever point she was at when her illness first began to preoccupy her. In most anorexics, that will be some time in her middle teens, just at the point when there is an enormous amount to be learned by interaction with her peer group. What this deprives her of is the time when she should be experimenting with social interaction. She should be learning how to function without her family to support her all the time; she should be using her peer group to discuss her social and emotional experiences; she should be experimenting with new situations and new experiences; she should be trying out various new ways of looking and behaving so that she can gradually find who she is and what she likes best. Eventually, from about 17 or so, she should be exploring the possibility of more intimate one-to-one relationships that in due course become sexual.

For even the best-adjusted and best-supported youngster this is a difficult time. There is an enormous amount of emotional growth and development to be made in a few years. Moreover, if the anorexic does not participate with her peer group in this development she will not only have missed out on it, but she will be at an age when it will be assumed that she has passed this stage.

Although Mary was 21 years old she had no interest in having a boyfriend. However, she liked the company of men of her own age and was friendly and open towards them. She was distressed and angry to find that for the men these friendships aroused sexual feelings, and that after a while they were no longer content to behave like her brother. She complained that men only wanted one thing, but she was utterly unaware of how her behaviour, in a woman of 21, was likely to be interpreted. Not only had Mary banished her own sexual feelings with her anorexia, she was blind to those of anyone else.

Some anorexics do marry or live with a partner in a sexual

relationship, but so far as is known the sex in these relationships is not usually satisfactory. It often seems that the anorexic woman feels nothing at all and cannot be responsive to her partner. Sometimes she experiences pain with intercourse as a result of extreme tension. Sometimes the couple make some kind of arrangement between them which results in the relationship being or becoming non-sexual. The man in such a partnership may himself have difficulties with his sex drive, or he may hope that in time things will change. When and if the anorexic woman recovers, these partnerships tend to split up.

POWER AND PERFECTION

Those around the anorexic often become frantic at her removal of herself from ordinary life and ordinary relationships. Families and friends become distraught as they see the one they love disappearing, in every sense of the word, right in front of their eyes. They cannot understand how she can so thoroughly deny ordinary, common-sense, everyday needs for food and rest, for companionship and comfort. Their incomprehension is often accompanied by irritation and anger. They have been made powerless by the anorexic and feel controlled and outwitted. As the anorexic becomes physically weaker, their anger is replaced by fear. This game, this style, this behaviour, can end in tragedy.

In contrast to those around her, the anorexic usually stays perfectly calm and somewhat remote. She does not seem to be able to understand what all the fuss is about. She will often continue to insist that she is fat even when she is dangerously emaciated, and the thinner she gets the more irrational she becomes. It is now thought that starvation affects a person's capacity to think properly and the starving anorexic certainly shows no sign of being able to grasp the danger that she is in. On the contrary she often feels fine and very few anorexics try to find help themselves; mostly they are unwillingly brought to help by other people.

The fact is that while the system goes on working the anorexic feels not only fine but wonderful. She feels powerful, triumphant, excited. Her bid for power over herself and her needs has succeeded. She is on the way to perfection. She often feels contempt for those ordinary mortals who need to do things like eat and rest. She is not like that; she is in control.

THE EFFECTS OF ANOREXIA

There are some anorexics who can achieve an equilibrium, maintaining this system for years or even, occasionally, for a lifetime. But they are fairly rare. Some seem to get better spontaneously without any help from anyone, but others become steadily thinner and thinner and more and more unwell. They are starving, and starvation progressively leads to the body ceasing to function properly. Chronic severe constipation is one of the first results of a diet that does not contain enough bulk. Anorexics sometimes eat bran in large quantities in an attempt to deal with this problem.

One of the most obvious and more serious signs of this process is the reduction and eventual stopping of menstruation, or the failure to establish menstruation at all. In more advanced stages of the disease there can be hair loss, the growth of lanugo all over the body, a permanent feeling of being cold and the unseen development of thinning of the bones – a precursor of osteoporosis. There will also be progressive physical weakness, which will eventually overcome even the iron control of the sufferer. All these are the natural results of chronic starvation.

It is this desperate state of affairs that will eventually bring the severely ill anorexic to medical attention.

CHAPTER 2

What is Bulimia?

I plan binges, and I always have one on the train on Friday afternoon on my way back to Nottingham where my mother lives. It's not really that I enjoy it but it's like a compulsion that I have to do it. I hate myself for it, because it's so disgusting, but in a weird way when I've binged and been sick I feel better. Sometimes I use laxatives as well and then the cramps in my guts and getting rid of all that shit makes me feel good too. It makes me feel I'm mad. I could never tell anyone about it.

It's disgusting! I've heard her doing it during the night. She goes to the kitchen and eats a whole load of stuff. I think she eats cereal mostly because I know she buys big packets of it and there's never any left. I think she makes toast as well because I sometimes hear the toaster popping. She makes a lot of toast, I can tell you. Then when she's finished she goes to the bathroom and sicks the whole lot up. I've decided to move out of the flat next month because I can't stand it. She's weird.

THE CLINICAL DESCRIPTION

Although it is known that bingeing and vomiting was practised among the Romans, it has not been noted in the medical literature in the past in the same way as anorexia. In fact it has only been described as an illness of young women since 1979, and was then thought to be extremely rare. Since then attempts to define it have continued and developed, and as with anorexia, there has been some interest in whether bulimia might have an organic, metabolic or genetic cause. Like anorexia, however, research so far has identified it as a psychological illness.

The definition according to the American Psychiatric Association is as follows:

Diagnostic criteria for bulimia nervosa

1 Recurrent episodes of binge eating (rapid consumption of a large amount of food in a discrete period of time)
2 A feeling of lack of control over eating behaviour during the eating binges
3 The person regularly engages in either self-induced vomiting, use of laxatives or diuretics, strict dieting or fasting, or vigorous exercise in order to prevent weight gain
4 A minimum average of two binge eating episodes a week for at least three months
5 Persistent overconcern with body shape and weight
(*DSM-III-R, American Psychiatric Association, 1987*)

There is a range of accompanying characteristics that may also occur with bulimia, depending on the means chosen to get rid of the food that has been eaten.

- damage to tooth enamel (as a result of persistent vomiting)
- digestive disorders
- irritation of the throat and mouth
- mineral imbalance
- loneliness, social isolation
- low self-esteem, self-hatred
- shame, self disgust

It is useful to distinguish between bulimia in two different groups of people.

Bulimarexia

As its name suggests this word describes the anorexic who has turned to bingeing as a way of dealing with the recurrent violent hunger pangs she feels, and then goes on to vomiting or purging as a way of keeping her weight at very low levels so that she gets rid of anything she eats. This is probably physically the most dangerous and life-threatening of all the eating disorders. The sufferer is coping not only with the effects of starvation but additionally imposes on her body the huge strains of bingeing and then purging or vomiting. The binges for an anorexic may not be very large – but they may also be excessive. It is not difficult to imagine the gross discomfort and danger of binging to someone who has been living on a very restricted diet. What is much harder for the sufferer to bear is the shame of having lost control.

> A 'good' day for Jane was a day when she was 'in control'. On 'good' days she would eat her very limited diet of about 800 calories, consisting largely of fruit and vegetables. A 'bad' day, and there were lots of them, was a day when she binged and vomited and used laxatives. On those days she went to the shops and brought home bread, cake, cereal, biscuits – all the food that she thought of as bad – and spent the next several hours alternatively bingeing and vomiting.

There are some researchers who think that bulimarexia should not be distinguished from anorexia, on the grounds that the sufferer's state of mind and world view is the same as an anorexic's. In the older literature, written before bulimia had been clearly identified, it is described as a possible aspect of anorexia. However I feel there is a crucial difference between the person who can maintain starvation without acknowledging need or hunger at all and the person who may *want* to do that, but who is in fact to some extent unable to deny her needs so completely. Psychologically the bulimarexic may be more approachable than the starving anorexic, although physically she may be at great risk. She may also be at risk psychologically, since her bingeing is the proof that her control system has failed. For this reason she may become seriously depresssed and suicidal.

NORMAL-WEIGHT BULIMIA

Although this group of people is as obsessed with weight and size as the anorexic they maintain their weight within the normal range. For that reason this is the most secret of all eating disorders because it does not show on the outside. Bulimics can often eat normally in public and even eat a normal diet, using their binges for relief from extreme tension. However, their eating behaviour can be as bizarre as any anorexic's in the more advanced stages of the illness. Many bulimics have no ordinary or regular pattern of meals. Their food intake is governed by whether they are bingeing or recovering from a binge. Their behaviour fills them with shame and disgust, but they are afraid to give it up because they believe that they would become enormously fat.

> Kate had worked for ten years in the fashion industry and was very conscious of the image that her job demanded. Her boss had once said that he would not have anyone larger than a size 12 working for him and Kate had taken that as some sort of threat. In her mid-twenties she had been that thin, although she was 5ft 8in (1.7m) tall, but as she became older and had two children she found it impossible to maintain that weight. She started using laxatives and before very long was afraid to eat anything unless she knew she could 'get rid of it' later.

INCIDENCE OF BULIMIA

The incidence of bulimia nervosa is as hard to estimate as that of anorexia. Conservative estimates suggest that it affects about 1–2 per cent of the female population between 15 and 45; bulimia tends to start in later teenage years and is present among older women in a way that anorexia is not. However, it is virtually certain that it is much more common than these figures suggest, and much more common than anorexia. Some studies of student populations have suggested an incidence as high as 20 per cent. Studies which stick closely to the precise diagnostic factors laid down by the American Psychiatric Association tend to produce lower figures but, as with anorexia, they ignore those with milder forms of the condition. Normal-weight bulimia is very hard to detect if it is not disclosed by the sufferer, so for this reason alone it is likely that many sufferers never receive any help.

As far as we know at present, there are even fewer men with bulimia than there are with anorexia.

Mortality rates are estimated to be about 3 per cent.

BINGEING

The need to binge is not something that any bulimic feels calm about. It is an urgent and compelling need that can either come over a sufferer suddenly without warning or be planned for hours or days ahead.

The bulimic who plans ahead will often make a special shopping trip for food, sometimes going to shops away from where she lives or works out of fear that someone may guess her secret if she shops repeatedly in the same place. She may go from shop to shop accumulating what she plans to eat. A great deal of tension and excitement can be created by the planning of a binge and a lot of thought can go into it. Some bulimics use marker foods, such as beetroot, so that they will know when they have vomited up everything they have eaten. Many have favourite bingeing foods such as crisps and biscuits which need no preparation and are easy to eat; however in the frenzy of a binge some people will eat food as unappetizing as raw spaghetti.

Sometimes the urge to binge is so pressing that it has to be met immediately.

Linda had gone right down one side of the High Street and up the other, going into every newsagent and general store and buying chocolate or biscuits in each one. As she walked between the shops she tore the wrappers off what she had bought and crammed as much as she could into her mouth before she went into the next one.

When the urge to binge takes over in situations where it is not easy to get food, the craving and desperation will over-ride the need for secrecy and discretion.

Mollie shared a flat with two other girls. They each had a shelf in the food cupboard and a shelf in the fridge. Mollie kept almost no food in store in an attempt to prevent herself bingeing. Her logic was that if she had no food to binge on, then she would not binge. Unfortunately it did not work that way. When, late at night, Mollie felt a desperate urge to binge, she would take her flat-mates' food, hoping that they would not notice before she had a chance to replace what she had eaten.

Bingeing often takes place in the evening and virtually always when the sufferer is alone, although some researchers have reported college students organizing group binges. A common scenario is for a bulimic to arrive home after a day's work to an empty house or flat. She may have bought binge food on the way home or she may use what she can find to hand. Either way, getting home seems to act as a trigger to an evening spent bingeing and vomiting, trying to deal with the events of the day with food.

Others spend whole days repeatedly bingeing and vomiting, while those who are more bulimarexic may treat almost anything they have eaten as a binge and attempt to force it out of their system. It is clear that these behaviours have nothing to do with the ordinary response to the physiological need for food.

Patricia finally looked for help when she realized that she felt guilty about eating anything at all without getting rid of it again, and was starting to limit even how much liquid she took in.

Buying a lot of food for binges is expensive and bulimics sometimes get themselves into financial difficulties because they spend so much on food. This can cause tension with others.

> Nancy's parents could not understand why she was always short of money when she was earning a good salary as a manager and had only herself to support. When she asked them for a loan to pay the rent they started to ask her a lot of questions about what she did with her money. Nancy felt totally unable to tell them that she was spending several hundred pounds a month on food. As she said, she might just as well flush the money down the toilet, and how could she expect her parents to understand that.

Some women steal, sometimes because they are short of food, but sometimes even when they have money. This stealing is often inexplicable to the woman herself, but it is at least partly to do with the secrecy and excitement of bingeing.

> Olivia was terrified of being caught shoplifting but could not stop herself from taking packets of biscuits from her local mini-mart. She complained that the security system was so poor that it was an invitation to steal, but she kept going back.

AFTER THE BINGE

Once the frenzy and excitement of the binge is over a bulimic is likely to be overtaken by feelings of panic. She may have taken in thousands of calories, yet she is a woman whose conscious wish – indeed her preoccupation – is with losing weight. How can she have let herself get so out of control? What can she do to ensure that despite taking in so much she does not gain weight?

In addition to her panic and guilt, she probably feels bad physically. Eating a lot of food quickly makes one feel acutely uncomfortable, especially in the stomach and abdomen. There are terrible accounts of people who have eaten so much in a binge that some part of their digestive system, stomach or throat, has ruptured, causing death.

Fortunately few bulimics go to quite such extremes, but they are nevertheless desperate to find a way of relieving the discomfort. Even a bulimarexic who has eaten no more than an ordinary amount of food may experience the bloated feeling which comes from eating any significant amount of food after a period of deprivation.

The emotional effects of a binge are often as bad, if not worse. The bulimic feels bad, guilty, weak-willed, out of control, disgusting, ugly, fat. She blames and hates herself for behaviour that she has not been able to control and which makes no sense to her. Her over-riding need is to undo what she has just done.

Having concentrated all her energy on taking food in, the sufferer now focuses just as singlemindedly on how to get it out of her body. Probably the most common method is self-induced vomiting. Sufferers put their fingers down their throats and make themselves sick. Some bulimics have become so used to doing this that they can vomit at will, without even having to stimulate the vomiting reflex. Others, worryingly, get to the point where they find it hard to keep food of any kind down, so used have they become to eating and then vomiting.

Understandably, this vomiting does not make a sufferer feel good physically. Being sick is a strain on anyone's system and tends to create an increased heart rate followed by symptoms similar to those of shock: sweating, shivering and weakness. This sort of physical stress following the physical and emotional stresss of a binge makes a normal-weight bulimic feel ill and exhausted, but is even more of a strain on the already weakened system of the anorexic.

Other bulimics will use laxatives as well as or instead of vomiting. Quite often this is how the bulimia is discovered – somebody finds the packets of laxatives. Overdosing on laxatives is common. There are many reports of bulimics taking more than 100 laxatives at a time. The stomach cramps and diarrhoea caused by laxative abuse are truly dreadful, and make it impossible for the bulimic to leave the house or to carry on with her normal day's activities. Laxative abuse is also dangerous in that it leads to an electrolyte (mineral) imbalance in the body which can result in collapse and even death. At a less dramatic level electrolyte imbalance routinely causes either dehydration or bloating because the fluid balance in the body is disrupted.

A third option which is sometimes used on its own or in combination with vomiting and purging is for the bulimic to compensate for her bingeing by starving herself.

THE CREATION OF A CYCLE

The experience of a binge followed by some method of ensuring that the food does not create weight gain does not usually engender the same kind of triumph and feeling of satisfaction that the anorexic experiences. On the contrary, the binge is experienced as a loss of control whose effects have only narrowly been avoided. Added to that, many bulimics feel guilt, disgust and remorse. They swear that they will never binge again.

However, the bulimic, especially the bulimic who has anorexic tendencies, very often sets herself up physically as well as emotionally for another binge as soon as the first one is over. Her binge eating has made her fear weight gain more than ever; what is more, she is horrified by her capacity to binge when she is consciously preoccupied with controlling her food intake. Her response is to attempt to strengthen the restrictions and controls she puts on her eating even more now that the binge is over.

For many bulimics it seems as though there is no third possibility between bingeing and starving. She commonly puts herself on a strict diet, or even stops eating altogether. However her body responds to this harsh treatment with cravings and desperate urges to eat, which she tries to ignore until they can be ignored no longer and another binge takes place. Obviously there is more to bulimia than this, for otherwise it would be extremely easy to correct the cycle, but there is undoubtedly a physical component which helps to maintain the pattern.

THE CONFUSION OF FEELINGS IN BULIMIA

We have already seen how the anorexic maintains her pattern of starvation by denying the physical feelings of hunger, and how she is expert at refusing to acknowledge her physical need for food or often also rest, warmth and so on. The bulimic is not able to maintain the total denial of ordinary need that rules the anorexic's life. Many bulimics have been anorexic and have progressed to bulimia. In a way that is psychologically healthier, she finds herself giving in to feelings of need but only to deny and undo them as soon as she can. Many bulimics admire the anorexic's 'control' and would like to be able to do the same. For them the acknowledgment of need which is symbolized by bingeing has still to be undone, removed, destroyed as soon as possible.

What is clear is that the whole cycle of bingeing and purging takes place with very little reference to ordinary feelings of hunger and the need to satisfy it. Bulimics are very confused about what they feel and often do not know whether they are hungry or full. This confusion makes it difficult for them to respond appropriately with their eating behaviour. With them it is truly a feast or a famine.

THE BULIMIC SYSTEM

This pattern of violent alternation between the feeling of need and the wish to deny it is also a system which extends to other parts of the bulimic's life. One area that tends to be affected is money. We have already seen how bingeing itself can create financial problems, but often the bulimic's finances will be permanently in a state of chaos for reasons other than her spending too much on food.

> Rosie loved clothes and was very interested in fashion. She often went to London's Oxford Street on a Saturday and spent hours window-shopping. She liked to be sure that the things she bought were exactly right and that she paid the lowest price she could for her clothes. Since she did not have much money, this made a lot of sense. What she never talked about was the times when she would suddenly abandon all her care and spend far more than she could really afford on clothes that she frequently felt later that she didn't really like. She spent a lot of her life worrying about how she was going to get out of the financial muddle that these 'binges' caused.

Cigarettes, alchohol and drugs are all substances with which the bulimic can find herself acting out the same patterns as with food, and in the same way vowing never to let herself do it again. Some researchers talk about an addictive or multi-impulsive personality to describe the person who acts out enormous needs and hungers only to regret or deny them immediately afterwards. Sometimes a person who is this unhappy will also harm herself by cutting or scratching herself, often on the inner arm or thigh. She may even burn herself. At the time, she does not seem to feel the pain as much as would be expected, but the action seems to relieve some unbearable tension in the same way that bingeing does.

The contrast between control and lack of it can also extend in more general ways into a bulimic's life. One aspect is the contrast between order and disorder in her surroundings.

> For weeks at a time Sarah could keep her room in the student hostel where she lived clean and tidy. In fact she tended to be rather obsessive about having things in exactly the same place and not going to bed before she had tidied her books and papers and put away her clothes. However, every so often her system would break down disastrously so that she gradually found herself living in complete confusion and disarray. Then by a heroic effort she would spend a day clearing up, won-

dering how she could possibly have allowed herself to descend into such a mess, and resume her patterns of total order.

Relationships and sexual behaviour can also be affected by the bulimic system.

> Tania spent long periods without having much of a social life at all, but she was worried by her capacity for one-night stands with men that she picked up in a club. She knew that what she did was not sensible or safe, and also that she got very little satisfaction from these encounters, but at the same time she found herself repeatedly enacting this pattern. 'I feel like Jekyll and Hyde,' she said. 'There's a part of me that I don't even recognize.'

The key words then for the bulimic, as for the anorexic, are need and control. An anorexic lives out a system in which needs, wants, desires and feelings have all been abolished. The logical end to this process is death, since it is impossible for any of us to go on living unless we are prepared to accept our needs. For her the needy part of herself is utterly unacceptable. She only likes and approves of the needless self.

A bulimic person, however, alternates between a 'good' self of which she approves, which has usually been disciplined to have few very well-controlled needs or feelings, and a 'bad' self that is full of overwhelming needs, desires and feelings. Neither she nor the anorexic can see that their needs are normal and that if they were given their normal space they would not be so troublesome. Both of them feel that their instinctual self is a monster of need and greed that must be disciplined, punished and restrained as much as possible. And of course both of them, by denying normal needs, turn them into violent cravings which devour time and energy.

The need for help is not immune from these systems. The anorexic finds it almost impossible to recognize that need, at least to begin with. The bulimic feels the need only to regret having asked for it. As a therapist I have many times been telephoned by a person complaining of bulimia who has made an appointment to see me and then not kept it. However, in time a bulimic can usually understand that she needs to know what is going on with her and can stay with that need long enough at least to begin to meet it.

SECTION TWO

What Causes Them?

CHAPTER 3

Anorexia and Bulimia as a Way of Coping with Life

At first glance it seems ridiculous to think of anorexia and bulimia as ways of coping. The distress and anxiety they cause both to sufferers and to those around them suggest that they are in fact ways of *not* coping. They create all kinds of terrible emotional and physical effects. A sufferer from either condition is likely to feel bad about herself, be preoccupied with issues of food, weight, shape and size to the exclusion of almost everything else, not enjoy a satisfying social life, find her close relationships seriously affected by her preoccupations, and not be able to work to her full potential. Physically she does not feel well a good deal of the time, is often weak and tired, suffers from problems with her digestive system and is physically uncomfortable much of the time. Some coping mechanism!

What is more, her physical condition, her social isolation and her strange, obsessive behaviour cause enormous anxiety to those close to her. Family and friends are often driven frantic by the stress of dealing with her strange and frustrating ways.

Despite all this, a sufferer finds it extremely difficult to give up her obsession. Research suggests that where anorexia and bulimia are serious enough to meet the clinical diagnosis, they are likely to persist for years; and the longer they continue the harder they are to recover from.

Yet to the outside observer nothing could be simpler: all

the sufferer has to do to be completely well is to eat properly! The fact is that although both of these conditions have been extensively researched and a great deal written about them, there is still a lot of ignorance and misunderstanding about them. The sufferers are often given very little sympathy. Sometimes people's reaction is one of downright hostility.

For these reasons when a sufferer first looks for help, whether from friends and family or from her doctor, she is likely to be given at best a lot of common sense and well-meant advice which boils down to: 'Why don't you just give up this foolish behaviour', or even sometimes a much more aggressively expressed order to 'Stop it!' But that is exactly the sufferer's problem: she does not know why she does not just give it up and she cannot stop it. Why not?

THE SEARCH FOR A PHYSICAL CAUSE

Following a medical model many researchers have looked for the answer to both anorexia and bulimia in some physical malfunction that creates these conditions. The great problem with such a hypothesis is that both conditions have not only become much more common in a very short time, but they are mostly found in developed industrial countries and are very much more common in young women than any other population group. These factors together make it unlikely that the disorders have a physical cause. Attempts to identify physical factors that might be responsible, such as the hypothesis that anorexia might be the result of zinc deficiency, have not so far provided any answers that have stood up to close examination. However, it should be borne in mind that it often takes many years to identify physical causes of illness and that physical and especially genetic factors cannot be entirely excluded as being wholly or partially responsible for anorexia or bulimia.

A PSYCHOLOGICAL APPROACH TO UNDERSTANDING

The alternative to a physical cause for anorexia and bulimia, and the hypothesis which currently commands most agreement among clinicians, is to see these conditions as having a psychological meaning and purpose. This meaning is certainly concerned with the individual and her family, but it is also concerned with the culture and society in which she lives. In this chapter I will discuss what anorexia might mean in terms of the emotional history of a sufferer and her family, and in the next I will go on to talk about social and cultural meanings in a broader context.

The underlying idea behind these concepts of psychological meaning is that anorexia and bulimia are functional – they are intended to accomplish something other than their avowed purpose, which is to be thin. If you ask an anorexic or bulimic girl why she misuses food the way she does, she will tell you that all she wants is to be thin. If she were thin, she says, everything would be wonderful. But this is patently untrue. For a start, she is already thin, very thin, while maintaining, in a way that is not reasonable to the ordinary person, that she is fat. The normal-weight bulimic is just that – a normal weight. If she really wanted to be thinner she would need to find some other way because the one she has chosen, for all its agony, simply keeps her at a normal weight. In other words, viewed in a strictly logical way, both the anorexic and the bulimic have put themselves in a position where they never achieve what they say is their goal. The anorexic can literally die of starvation, proclaiming to the bitter end that all she wants is to be thin; while the bulimic can destroy her health saying exactly the same thing while remaining the same weight – vomiting and purging are rather inefficient ways of ensuring that calories are not absorbed. The conclusion seems obvious: bulimia and anorexia are not simply about food and not simply about being thin, whatever the protestations of the sufferer.

No one would ever consciously choose to have either anorexia or bulimia; they are such dreadful afflictions and cause so much suffering. It follows that they must serve a purpose, some other purpose than the quest for thinness, and that purpose must be very important and also one that cannot be met in any other way – or at least that is how the sufferer must, at some level, understand it. What could this underlying purpose possibly be?

OBSESSIONS AND THEIR USES

The most obvious thing about anorexia and bulimia is their obsessive quality. Thoughts of food, weight, shape and size are constantly with the sufferer. Those in more advanced stages of the condition have difficulty in thinking about anything else at all. It is this which cuts them off from their friends and family and which can eventually make it impossible for them to study or work. In fact one of the signs that a young woman may be beginning to look for a way out of her prison is when she becomes fed up with thinking and living food, weight, shape and size all day, every day.

> The first thing that Valerie said when she joined the self-help group was that she was 'sick to death' of weighing herself and counting calories.

To the observer then the terrible thing about anorexia and bulimia is how obsessive the sufferer becomes and how little able to focus on anything else but food, weight, shape and size. However, perhaps it is precisely the distracting and preoccupying quality of these conditions that are most valuable and useful to the sufferer. Perhaps anorexia and bulimia are a protection against, or a way of coping with, whatever is worrying her.

This same argument is used in thinking about any obsession and how to respond to it. For example, a person who is obsessive about cleanliness will swear that all she is concerned with is that the house should be clean; but just as thin is never thin enough, so clean is never clean enough. The obsessive cleaner is just as capable of making the lives of those around her a misery as the anorexic or bulimic. It is plain in both cases that the sufferer is worried, anxious, tense, unhappy about something, but equally it seems clear that the worry cannot really be just about thinness or cleanliness. It is rather a way to stave off hidden anxieties.

It seems most likely that anorexia and bulimia are ways of dealing with difficult thoughts, feelings or memories.

> Wendy sat in the counsellor's office. They had started to talk about a very unhappy time in Wendy's life. After a few sentences Wendy stopped talking. She seemed very tense and anxious. After a few minutes the counsellor asked what was going on in her mind. 'I'm not thinking about that any more,' said Wendy. 'I'm thinking about what I'm going to eat this evening.'

Such direct awareness of the process is rare, but it seems likely that this is what happens a great deal with anorexia and bulimia, and in this sense they are ways of coping. The question that remains is what it is that needs to be defended against in such a desperate way.

WHEN AND WHY THE OBSESSION STARTS

One of the most useful ways for a sufferer to start to think about the meaning of her anorexia or bulimia is for her to ask the question: 'When did this all begin?' A very high proportion of sufferers seem to be able to date the onset of their difficulties from a specific upset or trauma in their lives. These can differ greatly from one person to another. The list below comes from my clinical experience and is by no means exhaustive:

- the death of a parent
- the illness, mental or physical, of a parent

- the death of a sibling
- the death of a grandparent who has been close
- the divorce or separation of parents
- sexual abuse
- rape or sexual assault
- leaving home
- the ending of a close relationship
- the loss of a close friendship
- examinations
- teasing or bullying

However, not all sufferers can identify a single incident or trauma which coincides with the onset of their problems. Sometimes that is because they do not take seriously what has happened to them, or because they are not consciously aware of its significance. Such a person will often deny outright that an event which coincides with the beginning of the disorder has any great importance. Sometimes this can be truly startling to the listener.

> Barbara had been rescued from a fire in her home by the fire brigade. The fire officers had had to use breathing apparatus to reach her and she had been extremely lucky to get out without suffering serious harm. Her bulimia had become a real problem to her immediately after this, but this coincidence meant nothing to her. She denied point blank that she had been scared by the experience, although she had been treated for shock in hospital. It was remarkable that Barbara was unable to allow herself to recognize what a dreadful trauma she had endured.

Some people cannot recognize what has happened to them because they are unaware of the effect on them of a series of stresses.

> Cathy went through a very unhappy time at school, when she was bullied over a period of about a year. Some attempt was made by the school to deal with the problem but Cathy's parents felt that Cathy ought to be able to manage the situation herself.
>
> At the end of that year her family moved and Cathy

changed school. In some ways this was a relief to her, but at the same time it meant that she had to try and make friends at a time in her school career when the other pupils were in long-established friendship groups. She became extremely lonely and withdrawn, and it was at this point that she started bingeing and vomiting. She could not understand how changing school could have triggered her bulimia, but began to see that it was just the last of a long series of stresses.

Annabelle's father had been in the army, and as a result the whole family had moved several times during her childhood. Every time she had had to adjust to a new house, a new place, a new school and to make new friends. Her bulimia started when at the age of 16 she was sent to boarding school. She liked the school, and had been sent there precisely to ensure that she had no more moves during her last two years at school, when she was preparing for exams, so it made no sense to her that her illness had started then. What she did not recognize was that this was not only the last in a long series of moves, but also one she had had to manage without her family beside her.

There are also a number of anorexics and bulimics whose illness seems to have been triggered not so much by a single event as by a continuing situation. Such situations can be obviously awful, such as sexual abuse or violence and conflict in the family. Others seem to be more to do with the sufferer feeling that she does not have the inner resources to be the person that other people seem to want her to be.

Dorothy came from a very strict religious family where extremely high standards of behaviour were required of the children. Any form of answering back or angry response from Dorothy to her parents was punished and she was required to be polite and smiling whenever she was with them. At the same time there were high expectations of her academically and severe restrictions on her social life. At the age of 14 Dorothy's lifestyle was significantly different from that of her peer group and she became anorexic.

In all these cases it seems likely that the eating disorder is being used as a way of dealing with the feelings that arise from situations that the sufferer finds it hard to manage. But there must be more to it than this. After all, many of these situations are ordinary life events that everyone has to deal with. Even when they have more dreadful traumas to cope with, not everyone suffers from eating disorders. Why is it that in some people they can trigger anorexia or bulimia?

HOW FAMILIES DEAL WITH FEELINGS

I think that the answer is very largely to do with whether a person has *needed* to adopt this mode of behaviour in order to deal with the feelings arising from her experience. Anorexia and bulimia are to a large extent afflictions of young women who are either still living with their families or have recently left them. They are usually still very much influenced by the family's way of doing things and especially by the family's way of dealing with feelings. This has an important role in the genesis of these conditions.

The events and situations that have been described above arouse very powerful feelings. As human beings we are made so that we can – and want – to manage our emotional experience by displaying and sharing feelings. A person who rarely does so, who seldom laughs or smiles, who does not cry or shout, who is not physically affectionate, is described as cold or unfeeling or remote. We are surrounded by media images of expressiveness and demonstrations of feeling; plays, books, films and videos all show us people reacting to situations by showing their feelings.

Not all families allow this. For different reasons, many discourage their children (and sometimes the adults as well) from openly expressing feelings, especially those that are negative or difficult, such as anger, disappointment, defiance, irritation or criticism.

There are many families in our society where there are very strict rules for controlling which feelings may be expressed by children and what modes of expression are permitted.

The controlled family

Elaine grew up in a family where there was a very elaborate but well-understood system involving who could express what feelings and how they could be expressed, although these rules were never directly acknowledged.

All members of the family were allowed to express good, happy and grateful feelings, although the children had to be careful that even those were expressed without making too much noise or disturbance. Elaine's father disliked the children displaying any feelings at all, even good ones, if he felt they were excessive. He was probably very much afraid of his own feelings and therefore afraid of everybody else's as well.

Elaine's mother had become expert at judging how much excitement or exuberance her husband could tolerate on any particular day before he would become angry. Elaine had also become expert as she became older. But her brother was not very good at judging this, and many family occasions were spoilt by her father's anger at her brother's excitement or loud voice.

When Elaine's mother was on her own with the children, much more open expression of excitement or pleasure was allowed by the children. But her parents could only display very mild feelings of pleasure or enjoyment before they became embarrassed and self-conscious.

Expressions of upset, such as crying, sulking, complaining or withdrawing, were allowed in some circumstances. Elaine's father could tolerate mild expressions of upset from Elaine for a short time, but could not allow crying from Elaine's brother.

Elaine's mother was not allowed to express any unhappiness about her father to him. She was allowed to complain about the children, although that was dangerous because he might deal with his difficulty in tolerating unhappy feelings in others by taking it out on the children.

Elaine's father was not allowed to cry, but he was allowed to complain and express disappointment both to and about all the other members of his family. None of them was allowed to disagree or protest about what he said.

Elaine's mother was allowed to complain about her husband to Elaine. This frightened Elaine, but she was not allowed to show it. On the other hand, Elaine's mother was not allowed to complain to Elaine's brother about her husband; he refused to listen. He also refused to listen if Elaine complained to him about anyone. He was not allowed to express any upset to Elaine; boys do not do that.

Both children were allowed to express their upsets on their own, so long as neither parent was required to be aware of it.

Expressions of anger were allowed only by Elaine's father when the family was together. He could be, and frequently was, angry with his wife and children when they were all together. None of them was allowed to be angry back or to have any other reaction except shame and apology for what they had done wrong. They were not allowed to indicate any other feeling by tone of voice or even by facial expression. Any attempt to do so was met with increasingly violent and intimidating behaviour from Elaine's father.

When Elaine's mother was with her husband, she was not allowed to express anger either, except about the children. This was dangerous, however, because he might take out his resulting anger on them. She was sometimes allowed to express anger about issues that had nothing to do with the family.

When Elaine's mother was with the children she was allowed to express anger to and about them. She also expressed anger to them about their father. In that situation they were allowed to express moderate anger about their father and mild anger towards their mother. Both of these reactions were dangerous, however, because they could upset their mother, which frightened the children.

The children were not allowed to express anger with each other in the presence of either parent. They were allowed to do so if they were alone together, but only on the condition that neither parent was allowed to know about it.

This example describes a real family, and it is not particularly unusual. It has its origins in the experience of the parents in their own families. As children, Elaine's parents learned from their parents which feelings they should be afraid or ashamed of. They are almost certainly reproducing the roles played by their parents and passing the system on to their own children. They have been taught to be afraid and ashamed of some feelings and they will teach their children the same lessons. With variations, such systems are rather common. Although there are severe limitations on what the parents can express, the ones who suffer most are the children. Their range of opportunity for the expression of feelings is very severely limited, but they also cannot be sure whether it is safe to express them and have to be careful of the feelings of their parents.

The 'nice' family

There are other kinds of systems which prevent or inhibit the free expression of a range of feelings. One of these is the 'nice' family. The 'nice' family finds it almost impossible to allow the expression of any feeling which is disturbing.

Mr Robertson was an accountant who lived a very regular and orderly life. He had always liked to come home to a tidy house and to find his wife and two girls waiting for him so that they could all have dinner together.

Mrs Robertson taught part-time at a local school and often deplored the behaviour of the children there. For a mild-seeming woman, it was interesting that she had no discipline problems with her classes.

Their two girls went to the local convent school, which had a considerable academic reputation. They were expected to work hard and were rewarded for high achievement. The convent was also well known for its tennis, and both girls had places on the team for their age group.

From the beginning the girls had been brought up in a rather strict and ordered environment. There was absolutely no doubt that they were loved and wanted, but they were also required and expected to conform to very high standards of behaviour. In the Robertson family no one ever raised their voice or shouted or swore. The girls were expected to give priority to homework, and their social lives were limited and controlled. Their parents made all their significant decisions for them, and many insignificant ones as well. Any sign of protest at this system was immediately squashed. Mrs Robertson had only to raise her eyebrows and say, 'I'm surprised at you!' for the protester to fall silent.

When the younger girl developed anorexia at 15, just as she was beginning her GCSE course, nobody could understand it. 'You are such a nice family,' friends and neighbours explained.

The Robertsons are also a real family and their system of dealing with feelings is also not unusual. None of the family members is allowed to express what is going on within them emotionally. It is as though all feelings that are the least bit difficult or disturbing are forbidden. What is rewarded is compliance with a family system of getting on with whatever duty or obligation is required, without protest or argument.

The family that has too much to cope with

Some families find it impossible to give enough attention to the needs of their children because the parents are already overwhelmed with what they have to deal with. They simply do not have the resources to take anything else on, with the result that the children are left to manage their feelings on their own.

Clare's brother Tom was born when she was four years old. He was a premature baby and for months it was very uncertain whether he would survive. He was kept in hospital in a special baby unit until he had put on enough weight to be allowed to come home. But it very soon became apparent that he had suffered quite serious brain damage.

The effect on Clare's parents was devastating. The strain of all the months Tom had been in hospital had taken its toll on them and now they were faced with looking after a baby who was seriously handicapped and would always require care. Gradually the family settled down to some kind of routine but Tom remained a huge concern throughout Clare's childhood. Her parents tried to give her some time on her own, but Tom's needs were a great strain on the family's physical and emotional resources. Clare learned that her parents needed her to manage as best she could because they already had enough on their plates.

THE EFFECTS OF A FAMILY'S FAILURE TO DEAL WITH FEELINGS

These sketches of family systems by no means cover all the possibilities, but they will perhaps be enough to illustrate the point that I want to make. When a young person finds herself in a system where, for whatever reason, her emotional needs cannot be met, it is not possible for her to process the ordinary feelings that are aroused by day-to-day events. From their earliest years the children of such families are trained to monitor what feelings they express within the family, and how they do so. The sanction for maintaining this system is the child's fundamental desire to win parental approval.

How are such children to manage their feelings if they are denied the normal means of open and straightforward expression and processing of them with a trusted person? The answer is that they will find other, less normal, less healthy and less direct ways of expressing them because, like water, feelings will somehow find a way out.

Youngsters will often be able to cope on their own without developing serious psychological symptoms of the strain, until they are faced by a situation that destroys their fragile equilibrium – one of the crises or critical life events listed earlier. Then the unvoiced feelings are likely to show themselves in other ways.

Typically, a boy will find ways of expressing them that are more or less delinquent, anti-social, defiant and external, and may include a wide range of behaviours, from outright criminal and violent behaviour to failure at school. The common denominator is likely to be that they involve and are aimed at targets outside the boy himself, especially other people and property.

A girl, on the other hand, will generally find ways of expressing feelings that harm no one but herself: depression, promiscuous sexual behaviour, self-harm and, increasingly over the past 20 years, eating disorders, including anorexia and bulimia.

FEELINGS THAT HAVE NO NAME

There are further problems for the person who has grown up in an environment where her feelings could not be expressed freely. She will not have learned how to identify and talk about feelings; in fact, she will have come to feel that she does not have them. The result is that she may find it exceptionally difficult to accept that she has feelings (especially difficult or negative ones) at all.

This is fairly typical of the anorexic, who often does not know what she feels, or even whether she feels anything at all. It is this confusion that makes it possible for her to deny her feelings of hunger. What this means, however is that not eating is only one aspect of the whole problem of being unable to identify feelings. An anorexic girl does not know that she is hungry, but nor does she know if she is angry or sad or disappointed. When she starts to eat more normally, her recovery is only beginning. She needs a whole education in identifying and expressing her feelings.

With the bulimic, the situation is rather similar. She knows she feels something, but she feels that she should not. She will also be very confused about what she feels and liable to identify any feeling (especially negative or difficult ones) as hunger, which she first resists and then succumbs to. Underneath this reaction lies despair of ever having her feelings met and rage that she is condemned to meet her ordinary human emotional needs with food. With a binge, she is attempting to satisfy an overwhelming need, which she calls hunger. But of course food will never satisfy her unmet emotional need. Similarly, it is her rage and dissatisfaction that causes her to regret her binge. The food has cheated and disappointed her and consequently she sets about trying to reverse the binge.

So the bulimic woman has two problems: first, she misidentifies what her needs are, so that her binges, whether on food, shopping or anything else, are not satisfying; and secondly, like the anorexic, she thinks she should not have needs anyway. Similarly then, stopping the bingeing and vomiting is the beginning of her recovery and she will feel much better as a result, but it is *only* the beginning and she too needs a whole education in the recognition of feelings and permission to satisfy them.

FEELINGS AND NEEDS ARE BAD

There is yet another problem for the anorexic and the bulimic, which is that they think that they are bad for having those needs and feelings that they do have. We are quick to learn from our environment and the earliest lessons we learn tend to be the most difficult to unlearn. An anorexic or bulimic woman has been taught that she should not have needs and feelings that her family cannot respond to. Unfortunately for her that does not make them go away, it merely represses them, and they are likely to surface from time to time. A young person does not know that this is normal and to be expected; she accepts the parental line that she should not have such feelings and consequently she believes that she is bad for having them.

The low self-esteem that is part of the personality of every anorexic and bulimic derives from this source. Their parents wanted them to be something that they were not and could not be – a person with fewer emotional needs.

They have tried to be that person and have failed. The anorexia and bulimia are heroic attempts to abolish feelings, but in the long term they do not work either. The woman with an eating disorder feels terrible about herself and sees no way out of the ghastly trap in which she finds herself.

CHAPTER 4

Cultural and Social Pressures

The last chapter tried to show the kinds of personal pressures that may lead to the development of anorexia and bulimia. What those personal factors do not explain is why a girl's distress should these days so often take the form of an eating disorder, or why eating disorders are overwhelmingly an illness of women rather than men. In this chapter I will try and identify the major cultural and social pressures that seem to have created this situation.

THE IMPORTANCE OF LOOKING GOOD

Since the Second World War, and especially since the 1960s, the developed industralized world has changed enormously. One extremely important aspect of this change has been the vastly increased prosperity of the large majority of the citizens of these countries. Talk to someone who grew up in the 1930s, or even the 1950s, and you will realize how much greater the economic resources and disposable income of huge numbers of people are. The development of the concept of the family holiday, for instance, is an indication of this change.

One of the results of this increase in economic resources has been the ability to acquire possessions in a way that is new in the history of the world. Never before has it been possible for so many people to own so much. We are all the owners of consumer goods on a scale undreamt of by former generations and still unavailable to the majority of the world's population.

This development has been sustained and enlarged by the advertising industry, which teaches us to want things and educates us about what we should want. But in case we might recognize that the acquisition of possessions is unlikely to make us contented or satisfied people if our deeper human needs are not met, advertising teaches us that our new possessions will bring us all those deeper things for which we long. 'Bring happiness home with new furniture now' is an old slogan and more obvious than advertisers would usually permit themselves to be these days, but it illustrates the trick that we allow to be played on us. We allow ourselves to believe that our deepest human needs can be met by possessions. And since those needs are hard to meet anyway, our gullibility is easy to understand.

But advertisers are not particularly wicked people who set out to delude and mislead us. They simply provide images that we already find seductive. Advertisers are the voice of a society projected on a billboard or a TV screen. The images can enlarge and extend our individual fantasies and desires, but they cannot create them out of nothing. They simply inform us of the value system that we already have.

So having money to spend and wanting to believe that buying things with it will make us happy, we are ready to accept the message the advertisers give us. If we buy things and create our lives in the image of the advertisements we will be happy. The creation of the personal image then becomes enormously important, even the most important thing in life.

Nowhere is this attitude more developed than in relation to physical appearance. It is decades since clothing was bought largely to satisfy the need to be warm and decent. Of course it has never been bought just for those purposes. The history of clothing as a means of display is almost as old as the human race, but when central heating keeps us warm and air conditioning keeps us cool, the utilitarian function of clothes diminishes. Then we can and do use them almost entirely for display. So minute details of clothing become important – such as the label, which has to do not with the use or function of the clothes, but with the creation of image.

Moreover, it is important to notice that the creation of the advertised image is not only to do with private and personal satisfaction, but provides a version of the self which gives us value and acceptance in the eyes of our peer group. These images differ according to gender, age and class, but they are very powerful within each group. The bizarre result is that gatherings of people from the same group can seem to be in uniform – for example the ubiquitous jeans and T-shirt worn by male teenagers. The drive to possess the acceptable image is strong. To be accepted and acceptable is one of the most basic human needs. 'Looking good' is then equated with 'being good', so that virtue and the image become the same thing.

THINNESS AS THE DOMINANT IMAGE

The dominance of the image has extended since the 1960s to the human body, especially the body of the woman. There is a right way for the female body to look and that way is thin. There are other desired elements of the acceptable image in relation for example to breasts, buttocks, legs etc, but by far the most important of these imperatives is the demand that the woman be thin.

This seems to be new. At other times – and indeed in other cultures today – the desired image of a woman is plump or even fat. Sometimes this is seen as an indication of prosperity, particularly in cultures where food is scarce; the woman who is fat obviously belongs to a family that is rich and has plenty of food. But it is also to do with fertility. As we have already seen, a very thin woman is an infertile woman. Many societies still require women to bear children and believe that fatness is an obvious indication that she can do so.

Even in more modern societies, such as 19th century France and England, paintings show that big women were seen as beautiful. It has often been remarked that in our own times even Marilyn Monroe was a size 16, which would not have made her acceptable to the post-sixties observer.

It cannot be doubted that the desirable shape for a woman in our society today is to be thin. How do we know this? Because we are surrounded by images of the female body and it is thin. From the vast range of sizes and shapes that the female body can assume, the thin, young woman is the one associated with the preferred lifestyles and images that are presented to us.

What is more, this image is not only presented for women's consumption and education – in the pages of women's magazines for example, or advertising products bought mainly or exclusively by women – but is also used to sell products bought by men. Not only are women taught how their bodies should look, so are men. It is interesting that men's bodies are very rarely used in this way, although the muscled and athletically developed young male is beginning to be seen advertising unisex products.

Women's history and experience have often identified them as existing only in relation to men – somebody's husband, somebody's daughter – and they have often been treated as the man's possession in law. Women have learned to make themselves agreeable to men on men's terms, so that their objectification in advertisements is not new. What *is* new is that the image that is now identified as pleasing to men and therefore makes a woman acceptable not just to herself but also to a man, is for her to be thin.

The great problem about this is that most women are not, and never will be, as thin as the images that are presented as acceptable in our society. The minimum requirement for the sort of model who appears on advertising hoardings is a height of 5ft 9in (1.73m) and a size 8 to 10. This shape will never be attainable by the vast majority of women.

For a start a woman's height and proportions are largely genetically determined, as is her weight. That is not to say that there are not considerable variations brought about by environmental influences. With better nutrition, for example, women are taller, have bigger feet, mature earlier physically and weigh more than they have ever done before. However, in normal circumstances, it is impossible to make permanent radical change in body proportions. To attempt to do so, as the 90 per cent of women who diet and then regain the weight loss plus a bit more can attest, is a waste of time. The sad result is that many women feel that they are unacceptable because they will never have the body shape that our culture demands of them. Anorexics and bulimics are among those who have not yet learned to accept themselves whatever the culture dictates.

THE FEEDER WHO IS NOT FED

Despite the impossibility of achieving it, the vast majority of women would like to be thinner than they are. A depressingly large number want that more than they want anything else in their lives. There are all sorts of sick jokes which provide a sidelight on this phenomenon: 'What are the three words a woman most longs to hear?' '"I love you?"' 'No. "You've lost weight."'

So, in pursuit of this goal, most women feel that they should deprive themselves of food, whether or not they actually do so. This creates a perpetual guilt about food and eating and a categorization of food into 'good' (low-calorie) and 'bad' (high-calorie). It leads to a sense of unworthiness that may be a pale shadow of the anorexic or bulimic woman's sense of not deserving to have needs, but is recognizably similar.

It is ironic then that most purchasing and preparation of food is done by women. Food is very largely a woman's territory; the responsibility for food and meals is usually hers, even if her partner helps by taking some part in the process. What is more, women are constantly being informed how to feed their families and urged to consider whether what they provide is good enough. There is nutritional advice and culinary inspiration in every woman's magazine and the overwhelming presumption is that the reader will be preparing food for others.

At the same time, often in the same publication, women are exhorted to eat less and to lose weight. Not for them the concern about whether they are satisfied or have had enough. That is for others. For themselves there is guilt and anxiety.

What is more, it seems that the limitation of a girl's intake and disapproval of a hearty appetite in a female begins in babyhood. Research has shown that girls are fed less than boys, irrespective of body weight and are trained from the very beginning to accept less. No wonder so many women find it difficult to identify hunger or fullness and have so little idea of how much food they want or need. These confusions are only greater, not different, in the anorexic or bulimic.

THE DIET INDUSTRY

There are murmurings here and there of a rebellion against the tyranny of thinness, but unfortunately this rebellion is only in its infancy. On the other side there is the vast machinery of the diet industry to encourage women to go on attempting the impossible. There is abundant evidence to suggest that the only way to achieve a normal and natural weight and way of eating is to be able to identify the feelings of hunger and fullness with which nature has provided us for exactly that purpose. However, most women have been socialized out of an accurate awareness of these feelings or any confidence in them.

Furthermore, many women use eating or not eating as ways of attempting to deal with their feelings and their emotional lives. This emotional agenda over-rides the ordinary regulatory mechanisms of hunger and fullness. Anorexia and bulimia are merely extreme versions of these rather common ways for women to relate to food.

Because of these confusions, women are vulnerable to the idea of eating in a mode specified by someone else, who knows what they should eat better than they do.

Moreover, the diet industry relies on women's alienation from their bodies to perpetuate myths about what diets can do for them. Women are intensively socialized to see themselves through the eyes of others. 'How do you think I look?' is a question that women often ask both men and other women. If pressed as to how *they* think they look, they will often express disgust with themselves.

A woman who feels this badly about her body will be willing to accept the basic premises of the diet industry: that fat can be lost from the body as if it were surgically removed and will not come back; and that long-term deprivation is both a good and a possible way to lose weight permanently.

In fact, continuing deprivation is likely to lead to the abandonment of the diet (which is what usually happens) or to the establishment of the binge/starve cycle that can become bulimia. In some people it leads to anorexia. The dieter, however, feels so little entitlement to what her body needs that again she accepts this premise.

Most of all, however, the dieter is willing to begin depriving herself and eating what somebody else tells her she should have because she believes that she is unacceptable. She has fallen for the great big lie that our culture sells her, that if she weighs less she will be more acceptable.

Ironically, this is happening at a time when women are actually growing steadily bigger and heavier and when the numbers of those defined as obese – more than 30 per cent heavier than average expected weight – has grown enormously. These women have responded to another message from our culture, which is that food and eating will make them happy. Advertisements for 'junk' food and confectionery frequently imply that eating the product will bring happiness. Overweight women are as much in the grip of our cultural fantasies as anorexics and bulimics, but they are physically less acceptable. No wonder that at any one time a majority of women is beginning, continuing or ending a diet. It is exceedingly painful not to be acceptable; no wonder they fall for the lie.

In the past this lie has been very cleverly and seductively sold by the diet industry. Users of diet products have been shown as not only thin but young, carefree and with attractive male companions. However one of the small signs of women's rebellion against the tyranny of thinness is that in the UK it is now forbidden to suggest in advertisements that the use of diet products will create happiness or success. This change has been bought with the suffering of women with eating disorders who felt themselves to be more than ordinarily unacceptable.

THE FASHION INDUSTRY

There are thus some small signs that things may be changing in relation to diet products, but this does not yet seem to be the case in the fashion industry. It is estimated that 47 per cent of the female population of the UK are size 16 or over, but you would certainly never know it if you went into the average high street fashion shop. In most of these stores 16 is the largest size available and there are four sizes smaller than that (8, 10, 12, 14). This is noteworthy not only because of the implication that any woman larger than a 16 is not expected to wear fashionable clothes, but also because such women simply do not exist as far as a large section of the retail clothing market is concerned. It appears that the cultural demand for thinness exceeds even the capitalist interest in profits.

WOMEN'S SELF-ESTEEM

What is sad, desperately sad, is that women are vulnerable to these messages and willing to be told that they are unacceptable non-persons because of their size. Sometimes when I run workshops I ask participants to brainstorm the words 'fat' and 'thin', producing lists of all the words they associate with 'fat' and 'thin'. They produce a stream of adjectives that reveal just how powerful these concepts are in our society. Here is a typical list:

FAT	THIN
gross	elegant
ugly	sexy
self-indulgent	attractive
flabby	weak
big	small
strong	pretty
heavy	light
hips	dainty
wobbly	pure
stupid	desirable
lazy	smart

This exercise engages people so much that I usually have to stop them – they do not run out of words very easily. Then just to make a point I ask the same group to repeat the exercise with the words 'short' and 'tall'. The difference in response is amazing. Although there are words associated with 'short' and 'tall', there are nothing like so many and they do not produce nearly the same passion or energy as the first part of the exercise. Yet logically there is no reason why we should not have a value system built on height. It would not be more ridiculous than the value system that our culture has built round weight.

How have women come to have such a poor sense of themselves that they are willing to be so deluded by all this nonsense?

The one thing that all those who work with women with eating disorders are agreed on is how poor their sense of self is. Women with eating disorders think that they are rubbish. They are full of self-hatred and self-loathing; they think that they are disgusting and that anybody who really understood how horrible they are would not want to know them. An anorexic has the sense of constantly repressing and denying the 'bad' part of herself to become more acceptable; the bulimic is engaged in the most violent fight with the 'hateful' part of herself that she cannot tame. But these are just extreme versions of a poor self-esteem that is exceedingly common among women. Why?

The people who have tried hardest to answer this question have been the feminist therapists, especially Orbach and Dana, whose work is listed and described in Further Reading. They have two lines of argument. The first is that the social education of women, inside and outside the family, undermines their confidence and sense of themselves from the very beginning. Women are thus always struggling with a deep sense of uncertainty and self-doubt. The second is that women are increasingly required to perform in the world and that their emotional resources are not adequate to manage what is required of them.

The social education of women

Some of the most important questions asked by feminists in the past 20 years or so have been: How do we grow up to be a man or a woman? What does that mean? What are we taught about what it means to be male or female? How are we socialized into our gender role?

Orbach's answer is that we are taught by our mothers and are prepared for our role in society by them. What they teach us is what they themselves have learned and penetrates far into our personality:

1 Women should mistrust their own spontaneity and energy and instead be careful and cautious. Boys are allowed and encouraged to have far more physical freedom than girls and are encouraged to take more risks. They learn to be much bolder, but they also have far more accidents. Girls are taught to be careful but also to be anxious and uncertain about their own capacities.

2 Women are taught not to be too needy. They receive less attention than boys both at home and at school, and they are taught to be patient in expressing their needs.

3 Girls are taught to defer to others, let others take the lead, defer to the opinions of others, place themselves in subordinate and auxiliary positions.

4 Girls are taught to anticipate the needs of others. Just as mothers anticipate the needs of babies and children, so their daughters are taught to be on the lookout for what others need, rather than focusing on their own needs.

5 A girl is taught to define herself in relation to others rather than in terms of separateness and independence as males are taught to do. They are taught to place a high value on compliance and conflict avoidance as ways of maintaining emotional connection.

This is a formidable list. At their best, many of these lessons teach women those virtues of collaboration and co-operation which seem likely to be crucial if the world is to continue to function. We are probably just beginning to understand how disastrous the male virtues of ambition, competition, aggression and individualism have been for our world. We are likely to need women's capacities for concern for others and awareness of the needs of others. At their worst, however, these lessons implant a tremendous sense of uncertainty and doubt in the girl's mind about what she is allowed to do and be and even what she is. It is not hard to see an anorexic or bulimic woman as having taken these lessons so much to heart that she feels that recognizing or attempting to meet her own needs is forbidden.

Carrying a full load but running on empty

We need to set against this account of the socialization of women their increasing participation in spheres of life and work that were previously reserved for men. Even though it would be untrue to say that women have equal opportunities with men, nevertheless there has been a huge development in their contribution to the paid workforce and their functioning in the world.

A very high proportion of women have some work outside the home and make a valuable and necessary contribution to the household economy. However their work inside the home and in childcare has diminished very little, despite these other obligations. All surveys show that women still perform by far the larger proportion of housework and childcare, even when they are living with a man. At the same time there is an increasing number of single-parent households where the single parent is the mother, who is resonsible for the entire care and support of the children.

Shirley Conran's book *Superwoman* was an early attempt to show women how to do the impossible and manage this heavy burden of work and responsibility, but women are still struggling with more work of all sorts than they can really manage. Most of them are putting a brave face on it and doing the best they can.

Younger women are the inheritors of this model, and the expectations of them are even greater than they were of women who grew up in the sixties and seventies. Far more of them go into further and higher education, and increasingly girls are out-performing boys at every educational level.

These demands and expectations are fuelled by images of women on television. In sport and dance, for example, we are shown examples of extraordinary achievements by (thin) women. This generates pressure and competition right down through the layers to the aerobics class held in the church hall.

Yet these demands and expectations are made of women who feel extremely fragile and vulnerable emotionally. Such women often talk about feeling fraudulent: they appear to do well and manage everything, while inside they feel hopelessly inadequate and useless. These are the women who can find themselves using anorexia and bulimia as a way of coping with what feels like the hopelessly undeserving, unentitled self inside.

There is no doubt that these cultural and social pressures create an emotional climate which predisposes women to the development of eating disorders. Fortunately by no means all women are overwhelmed by them. However, it is not hard to see that if there is a conjunction in a young woman's life of these cultural and social pressures with personal and family circumstances which offer her inadequate support, then anorexia and bulimia are not unreasonable responses.

Let us now turn to considering what can be done about it.

SECTION THREE

What Can Be Done To Help?

CHAPTER 5

Strategies for Self-Help

This chapter discusses ways in which a sufferer can help herself. The next describes and discusses professional help. How can you know whether a sufferer can help herself or whether she needs professional help?

It is possible to create a list of criteria to guide you if you are thinking of trying to help yourself.

1 You must be willing to admit that there is a problem. This is usually easier for a bulimic than an anorexic. Most bulimics do not enjoy their way of using food at all and hate the process of bingeing and vomiting. Most anorexics are reluctant to acknowledge that there is a problem because their starving gives them more psychologically.

2 You must be willing to begin to work on giving up your misuse of food. It is unrealistic to suppose that any anorexic or bulimic is 100 per cent or even 75 per cent willing to do so, but you must be 51 per cent willing. You must, at least for a significant proportion of the time, be more willing than unwilling. Any recovery is likely to have setbacks and delays, but a basic desire to recover will help you through these.

3 You must be willing to maintain the weight you are now and not try to lose any more while you are trying to recover. If your weight is dangerously low you will not be able to undertake a recovery programme on your own anyway. Both medically and psychologically you will be unfit to do so and you need professional help.

However, if your weight is low without being dangerous, or if it is normal, it is now thought to be possible to institute a recovery programme if you agree not to lose more weight. If that turns out to be impossible, then you need professional help.

4 You need a lot of support. It is ideal if your family is willing to help you both practically and psychologically. In a perfect situation you will be enormously helped if you and your family can think together about the contribution of the family dynamic to your illness. However, not many people are blessed with families that can take the opportunity offered by the illness of one of their members to grow and develop as people. Of those that can, most will benefit from professional help. However, do not dismiss your family as potential helpers too quickly. Read the rest of this chapter; suggest that they read it, and see if they are willing to take up the invitation to help you.

As well as considering whether you can get help from your family, think about the support you can get from your partner, if you have one. Some partners are so relieved that you are trying to deal with your difficulties that they will help in any way they can. Again, your illness can provide an opportunity for your emotional growth as a couple. Others are too scared to become deeply involved, although many will offer practical support and encouragement if asked.

Many women derive their emotional support in this, as in other matters, from a network of women friends. If your illness has not alienated you too much from your friends, and if you feel it is possible to admit your difficulties to them, they may well prove extremely valuable in your recovery. Few women in our society are completely free of problems about food and weight, so it is highly likely that even if they do not have such severe problems as you do, they will be able to empathize with your difficulties.

Even if you have no personal support system along

any of the lines described above, you may still be able to manage if you can find a self-help group (see the section on Useful Addresses).

It is also possible that you can find a concerned person who is not particularly close to you, who might be willing to help. I have known young women who have used a teacher for this purpose and sometimes their doctor or a member of a health centre team. Even if such people do not know much about eating disorders, they can listen and support what you are trying to do. If you are a member of a church, someone there may be willing to help.

Whoever you find, it would probably be useful to give them this book to read, so that they know what you have been thinking about. What you need from them is a non-judgmental, patient willingness to listen, to encourage and to support your efforts.

If, however, you do not have and cannot get any of these forms of support, I think it is unrealistic to believe that you will be able to heal yourself entirely on your own. It is probably because you are emotionally alone that you developed an eating disorder in the first place. You need a companion to help you out of it. If you have not got one to hand, think about finding yourself professional help.

5 Self-help is a more realistic option, even with support, if you do not have other significant psychological problems as well. If you are very depressed, if you harm yourself by cutting or hurting yourself, if you also have problems with drugs or alcohol, if you are a compulsive spender or gambler, then you need help from professionals. It is too much to ask of yourself that you sort out so much on your own.

USING THIS CHAPTER

If you are considering embarking on recovery without professional help, then I suggest that you read through this chapter to see the different aspects of recovery described. You can then think about what you are undertaking and begin to imagine what the process might be like for you.

I can only describe a limited amount in one chapter, so you may want to use some of the other books listed in the Further Reading. I have given a brief description of their content, which should help you to find what is of particular relevance to you.

Recovery will take time. After all, it has taken you at least months and more likely years to get yourself to where you are now. It will take months and probably years before you can say that you have truly recovered, not just from the food misuse, but also from the mind-set that goes with it. Recovery from the actual food misuse can usually be fairly rapid – it can happen within months. The undoing of the psychological systems that underlie the eating behaviour takes longer.

Recovery is work and needs space in your life. It cannot be done without devoting time and energy to it. But think how much time and energy you have devoted to your illness. Use the same amount of time and energy on recovery and you will soon be much better.

THINKING ABOUT RECOVERY

All recovery, whether with professional help or without it, is based on the same principles. Eating disorders of all kinds have received progressively more attention from clinicians over the past 20 years. Until comparatively recently there have been competing ideas about how to help the affected person. Now however, a consensus seems to be developing that sustained recovery depends on addressing three areas.

The behaviour

A bulimic is distraught about bingeing and vomiting, but may not want to give it up for a long time. Anorexics rarely want to give up their starving although they are often surrounded by people who want them to. Nevertheless, it is only when an anorexic or bulimic is of normal weight and can eat normally without distress or phobic reactions that she can be said to have recovered. The eating patterns must change.

The habits of thought

As we have seen, anorexia and bulimia are not just about patterns of food use; rather food use is the tip of the iceberg of a whole system or lifestyle. That lifestyle is sustained by a complicated belief system that includes such elements as:

- I am fat.
- Fat is bad.
- I am bad.
- I should not eat.

Cognitive therapy is a process of uncovering this belief system and trying to learn new patterns of thought. It depends on the person being able to see that these habits of mind do not make sense, and on her being willing to practise alternatives, even if they feel very strange to begin with. These habits of mind are not very easy to change because they feel as if they are true, but unless they are changed any weight gain or change in eating behaviour is unlikely to be permanent.

These first two aspects of recovery can stand alone and can be undertaken whether or not you continue to explore what brought you to misuse food in the first place.

The underlying feelings and emotional history

As will be plain from what I have already said, I consider that the roots of an eating disorder lie in the sufferer's family history and personal emotional experience. The eating disorder is designed to deal with the pain of that experience, but has itself become the problem and the pain.

The pain of the past limits many people's lives and potential, not just those with anorexia and bulimia. My conviction is that while we remain ignorant of what it is in the past that we are trying to deal with, we are condemned to spend too much energy protecting ourselves from that knowledge, and often repeating patterns of behaviour, learned in the past, that are harmful to us. Exploring our own history can liberate us from old habits and old ways of thinking that are no use to us in the present. Psychotherapy has as its fundamental aim an increase in autonomy and responsibility for ourselves.

There are therapists who think that if a person changes the eating behaviour and the distorted ways of thinking about food and weight, it means that the sufferer has recovered from an eating disorder. There are also therapists who think that if a person identifies the pain in the past that has brought her to adopt an eating disorder, then she will recover, without explicit attention to the eating behaviour and obsessional thinking.

I think that the fullest recovery, and a liberation from the eating disorder which will enable a sufferer to grow and develop most fully as a human being, involves all three. However this is an ambitious programme and there are undoubtedly sufferers who are content to have got rid of the worst manifestations of food misuse. It is my experience as a therapist that when somebody is not seriously unwell from the eating disorder and has some idea of why she might need it to help her cope emotionally, then psychotherapy, with relatively little attention to the behavioural and cognitive elements, will bring about a change in the eating behaviour and the distorted thinking as well as personal growth and development. Where anorexia or bulimia are more deeply entrenched, however, each of the three elements probably needs to be explored more thoroughly and given a lot of space.

CHANGING YOUR EATING BEHAVIOUR

This section requires you to summon up the adult, commonsense part of you that knows what is good for you and what you need. That knowledge has probably been hidden by all sorts of feelings as well as by poor eating behaviour, but it can be found in most anorexics and bulimics. If you are unable to make use of this first section of the self-help strategies, then you will probably need professional help with your recovery.

Working out a good diet

Many people with eating disorders have lost touch with what or how much they should eat in a normal diet. Some may never have known what a normal diet is, especially if they come from families where meal times were chaotic and unstructured. For others, memories of normal eating are so far in the past that they are unreal. All will be out of touch with the ordinary messages of hunger and fullness, appetite and satisfaction that are the body's natural guides to eating behaviour. These mechanisms will return in time, but first you will have to establish for yourself a pattern of normal eating, and you will have to do it from theory rather than from instinct since for the moment your instincts will not be working properly

The very idea of working out a 'proper' way of eating will almost certainly be frightening, so here we come to the first problem in recovery, one which you will have to struggle with many times: doing what you know you need to do, and what will be best for you, feels wrong and bad. It is at this point that you need the adult, commonsense part of you that can say to yourself 'Yes, I know this feels strange and bad and wrong. At the same time I know this is what I need to do to recover and with at least 51 per cent of me, I want to recover!'

When you feel particularly low or discouraged you can

perhaps also use those very problems that have brought you to this situation and say to yourself, 'Just now I find it hard to do this for myself, but I will do it for the sake of the people round me who love me and worry about me and want me to be well.'

So let us return to the task in hand. You must establish a normal pattern of eating because unless you do so you will not have recovered and you will not be able to give up your obsession with food and fat. However difficult this seems there is no escaping it.

I have never yet met a person with an eating disorder who was not an expert on calories and nutrition. Use this knowledge to devise sample menus for yourself. In the unlikely event that you do not have this information it is readily available in many guides and magazines. A woman needs, at a low estimate, approximately 2,000 calories a day, so work out an eating plan that provides you with about that number. Do it in the form of different things for breakfast, lunch and dinner, plus a list of possible snacks. Most people like to eat something about every two to three hours, and meals may thus be separated by snacks, so that you are eating approximately six times a day.

Make sure that you include in this list things that you like. There is very little point in including things you think you ought to have if you can't imagine eating them. To begin with you will probably need to be rather precise about what you prescribe for yourself: '2oz (57g) sugar-free muesli and 6oz (170g) semi-skimmed milk' will almost certainly feel better to you than just 'muesli and milk'.

If you have difficulty doing this exercise, try imagining that you are worried about the way your sister or your best friend eats and make the menus as if they were for her. (Here again you can use for your own benefit your knowledge of what other people need.)

By the time you have finished you should have collected at least five or six choices for each meal and a list of snacks. Any combination of these in one day should add up to about 2,000 calories.

Now find someone to whom you can show this meal plan and with whom you can discuss it. It does not need to be someone who knows as much as you about nutrition. The goal at this point is not to devise the perfectly balanced, nutritionally ideal way of eating; rather it is to find your way back to normal eating patterns.

It will help you to feel that your programme of recovery is real if you share it with someone who can support you each step of the way. So far you have not made any practical changes, but your planning is a way of signalling that you are trying to make those changes.

Comparing with where you are now

The next thing to do is to write down an account of a typical day's food use at the point you are now. This is not a very easy thing to do. It is hard to be really honest with yourself about how you use food, especially since you are probably always full of good intentions about changing what you do.

You may want to keep a record of what you do with food over a week. That is also a hard exercise because you will be rubbing your nose in your daily struggle. However, even the pain of doing this can be used to give you energy to change. If you can say to yourself something like 'Why am I doing something that causes me so much shame just to admit it to myself?', then that may provide you with extra impetus towards recovery.

It will be immensely useful to you if you can acknowledge to your supporter just how it is that you use food at the moment. Even though it may make you feel guilty and ashamed, it will also make it more real. People with eating disorders often manage to hide from themselves what they are doing to themselves. Admitting it to someone else can sometimes feel like waking up.

Once you have created an account of how you use food now, you will be able to compare it with the plan for

normal eating that you have already made. I will be surprised if you are not rather shocked, perhaps even frightened, by the difference between the two. Use this to help
you continue to the next stage.

Beginning to change your eating habits

You now need to make a timetable for the introduction of
this new way of eating. Of course it would be ideal if you
could make this change all at once, but if your eating has
been seriously disordered for a long time, then you may
need to do it in stages. So, starting with the part(s) of the
day when you think you will be most likely to be able to
change, set out a timetable for the way you are going to
proceed. The introduction of this new way of eating could,
for instance, develop in two-weekly stages:

Day one, week one: Begin eating normal breakfast and
mid-morning snack.
Day one, week three: Add normal lunch and tea-time
snack.
Day one, week five: Add normal dinner and late evening
snack.

This timetable, however, is something you will have to do
for yourself. Try and make as complete a plan as you can.
Your temptation will constantly be to give up on recovery.
The more you can help yourself with a firm structure, the
more likely you are to make progress.

   The actual implementation of the plan will be hard. You
will feel terrified that you are going to be monstrously fat;
you will feel sick, greedy, bloated – every bad feeling you
can imagine. But you will not become monstrously fat
from a regime of 2,000 calories a day. What is most likely
is that you will maintain the weight you are. If you are a
normal-weight bulimic you may lose a little, provided you
are not bingeing. If you are a low-weight anorexic you
may gain a little.

Try and use your support as much as you can, especially in this early stage. Share with at least one person your programme and the ups and downs in how you manage and how you feel about it. Allow yourself to be pleased with your daily success. Sometimes it can be fun to institute a reward system to measure your success – for instance a gold star for every day you manage to keep to your programme.

Conversely do not be discouraged by setbacks and failures. Sometimes we expect recovery to look like Concorde taking off – a smooth trajectory into the air. From what I have seen it is more like a journey along a rutted track with lots of jerks and lurches. What is important, however, is that you travel the road, not whether you get a bit shaken up in the process.

Let us now explore some of the potholes in the road.

Problems for anorexics

Perhaps what I have written about returning to normal eating makes it sound as though I have no idea of what a difficult task that will be for you. I think I know how hard it will be.

The problem for you is that you are planning and organizing a timetable for eating more food than you have probably done for a long time. There is no getting round the fact that this will be difficult. If it were easy you would have recovered long ago. However, you have said to yourself that with at least 51 per cent of yourself you want to recover, and you must therefore be a person with a strong will-power. Use that will of iron to help you recover! A book that you may find helpful is Marilyn Duker and Roger Slade: *Anorexia Nervosa and Bulimia: How to Help* (details in Further Reading).

There are a number of predictable ways in which these changes will be difficult for you.

1 You will feel physically uncomfortable when you eat even one meal and one snack in a day. This is because you are unused to putting food in your stomach, and your whole digestive system has grown unused to processing it. You are likely to feel pains in your stomach and abdomen, possibly colicky, crampy kinds of spasms. You will almost certainly feel uncomfortably full and bloated. Starting with food that is easier to digest, like yoghurt and honey rather than wholemeal bread and apples, may help a little. You can also use liquids, such as milk drinks and fruit juices, to help you. Try and think how you would help a dearly loved friend or sister back to eating normally and then treat yourself with the same kindness and compassion. In a relatively short time your digestive system will start to return to normal.

2 You will be tempted to make one meal last all day and not eat anything else. Steel yourself to continue with your programme of introducing three meals and three snacks a day.

3 You will feel tempted to make substitutions to reduce the calorie count of the meals you have planned for yourself. Keep reminding yourself that you are taking responsibility for your recovery. Let the adult part of yourself take charge of the scared child. Try and say to her, 'Yes I know you are scared, but this is for the best, and you must trust me to help you!'

4 You will feel afraid, terrified, every time you increase your food intake. Unfortunately there is no way of avoiding that. Use your support; stick to your scheduled plan of returning to normal eating. Use your great willpower to help you.

Problems for bulimics

So far I have not mentioned the main problem for bulimics: bingeing. That is not because I do not realize what a problem it is. However, you have to begin by thinking about a normal diet because without that you will not stop bingeing anyway. As I have already said, bingeing is caused partly by psychological and partly by physiological factors. Not having enough to eat and going without food for long periods are the physiological triggers. The ravenous hunger is at least partly to blame for bingeing (which is why so many anorexics eventually become bulimic). Start eating an adequate diet and you are at least one step towards in stopping bingeing. A good book for you to read is Peter Cooper, *Bulimia Nervosa: A Guide to Recovery* (details in Further Reading).

However there are also psychological triggers for bingeing aside from the physiological. By not eating normally you set yourself up for a binge, but then something happens that creates feelings in you that seem unmanageable – for instance, something makes you angry or upset or disappointed. Then you turn to food as a way of managing those feelings, and then regret it and vomit or purge yourself.

In order to stop bingeing you need to become more aware of the psychological triggers. The way to do this is to note when you binge and then go back over that day looking for the psychological event or the emotional experience that has hurt you or upset you.

This is difficult because the whole purpose of bulimia, as we saw in Chapters 3 and 4, is to protect you from feeling what you feel. However, if you practise, you will gradually become more aware of the system you operate. Treat the urge to binge as a signal that something has happened to upset you. Then try and use your supporter to share those feelings (perhaps by telephone if the urge to binge is strong), rather than acting on them.

Some therapists recommend having a list of distractions available to help you if you feel the urge to binge, especially active distractions. I think these can help in the short term, but the problem with them in my view is that although the urge to binge disappears because of the distraction, you will not have learned anything about the function of your system, so in that sense you are no further forward. On the other hand, if you get to know what situations make you feel like bingeing (eg pressure at work; quarrels/arguments at home; reminders of old hurts and losses; feelings of failure and inadequacy), then you at least have more of a choice about how to deal with those situations and feelings. Use your support in working on this issue.

CHANGING YOUR HABITS OF THOUGHT

This section is directed towards changing the characteristic habits of thought which accompany your illness. As an anorexic or a bulimic you will have developed a set of automatic ways of thinking which you repeat many times a day and which help you sustain your anorexia or bulimia. You may not be aware that you are doing this and you may be surprised to think that you are working hard at maintaining your eating disorder, but I am sure that that is what is happening.

In order to recover you need to do three things:

1 Discover what it is that you say to yourself.
2 Decide that you do not want to continue to repeat these messages.
3 Replace these old messages with new ones.

A simple example of this process at work might be:

1 Every time I think about eating a proper meal I say to myself: 'You don't need that, and if you eat it you'll get fat.'
2 I can see this message is not true; I do need to eat and if I eat regularly and carefully I will not get fat.
3 I will try and replace the old message by saying: 'I need to eat and eating normally will not make me fat.'

Identifying the messages

We are all talking to ourselves all the time, giving ourselves messages of all sorts. The task for you is to identify what messages you are repeating to yourself about food, weight, shape and size. Start making a list of what you habitually say to yourself in relation to these issues. Just by imagining yourself in typical situations (weighing yourself and finding you are a pound heavier, meeting a friend and being asked to go out to eat, waking up in the morning feeling hungry, etc), you can probably identify a good number of these messages. Make a list of them.

Then start consciously training yourself to listen for what you say to yourself when these situations arise. You may be surprised at how often you repeat the same messages. You may notice how harshly and violently you speak to yourself. You may start to realize how much energy goes into maintaining your system. Add the messages you identify to the list.

Reviewing and considering the messages

You now need to think about whether you want to persist in repeating these messages. They will reveal to you a value system based round a few core ideas that are likely to be something like this:

- Food is bad and dangerous.
- Eating is not allowed; eating is disgusting.
- Eating makes you fat.
- I am fat and ugly.
- Being fat is wicked and contemptible.

Just writing down these core beliefs may help you start to see what a limited value system this is, but try also using these methods of reviewing them.

1 Are these ideas always and in all circumstances true? When and with regard to whom might they not be? Would they be true for:
   • a baby
   • your mother
   • your best friend
   • a refugee
   • your child
2 In what limited circumstances and for whom might they sometimes be true?
3 Do other people have the same belief system? At all? To a limited extent? Ask your supporters whether they have the same belief system.
4 Think about the person you love most in the whole world. What are the things you love and value about that person? Do you love them mostly because they are thin? What does that mean? Do you think you have one value system for yourself and one for other people? Do you want to continue like that?

This value system has been built up slowly and carefully over a long time. It will not immediately disappear just because you start to identify it and start to want to change it. As I have stressed throughout this book, your whole eating disorder was developed for a purpose. It will take some time before you are convinced that you can manage without it. Typically it is the beliefs about yourself that are the hardest and slowest to change. Hating yourself and thinking you are horrible and evil is something you have been practising for years. It will take time to replace these messages of hate with messages of love and concern.

Replacing the old messages

There is a well-known book that you may want to look at to help you further with this part of your programme: Louise Hay, *You Can Heal Your Life* (see Further Reading for details). She discusses in more detail than I can here how to affirm what is good and positive. However, the system is basically very simple: it is to replace the old messages with new ones that are more creative and useful and that will not harm you in the way the old ones have.

Get out the list you made of the old messages and for each old message devise a replacement. So for example:

- 'Eating is disgusting' could become 'Eating is necessary'.
- 'Eating normal meals will make me fat' could become 'Eating normal meals will help prevent me bingeing'.
- 'I am fat and ugly' could become 'I am fine just the way I am'.

To begin with this will feel extremely difficult, especially because you will not believe these new messages. This is where many people trying cognitive therapy come to grief. The old messages *feel* true and so it is easy to go on repeating them. The new ones probably feel stupid and untruthful. But remember we are talking here not so much about feelings as about habits. You are retraining yourself to have a new set of automatic thoughts. Just think how tricky it is to do that when for example you change your telephone number; the old number sticks in your mind and it is a real effort to retrain yourself to remember the new number. Your automatic repetition of your belief systems about food, weight, shape and size will inevitably take some time to change.

KNOWING YOURSELF BETTER

I am convinced that the way we are and the way we behave have developed for very good reasons. I do not believe that any of us acts in ways that make no sense. Our logic is not always easy to understand, but with thought we will discover that what we do makes perfect sense according to our own individual logical system.

You, as a person with an eating disorder, are already familiar with this idea. After all if you are anorexic or bulimic you have been surrounded by people telling you your starving or bingeing makes no sense. Yet to you it has made perfect sense. To you, with your dreadful fear of fat, it has seemed quite logical to misuse food the way you have. However, if you have read this far, you will have at least the suspicion that there is something wrong with your logic.

But I would suggest that there is a deeper set of reasons, to do with your personal history, your family, your social and cultural environment, which means that it made perfect sense to have an eating disorder. For you in your situation, an eating disorder was a way of coping and managing, as I discussed in Chapters 3 and 4. Not only was it a way of coping, it was the best way of coping for you in that situation. You needed your eating disorder then. The fact that you now want to get rid of it suggests that you do not need it to anything like the same extent.

In the two previous sections of this chapter I described how you can go about changing your eating behaviour and your attitudes towards food and your body. In this section I suggest how you can start to make sense of why you needed an eating disorder to begin with. The point of this is not just to tidy up the loose ends of some sort of historical investigation, but to help you to be more aware, in the present, of what you have had to deal with and how you need to take care of yourself now so you will not need an eating disorder again in the future. It is also to help you see that in having an eating disorder you were trying to help yourself and that it made perfect sense for you in those circumstances. If you can allow yourself to understand that, you can also probably feel much more compassionate and forgiving towards yourself.

However, not everyone wants to or can conduct this kind of exploration or investigation. It is up to you to decide how far you want to go with the various strategies suggested and use those that seem best for you. You can also decide the timing. The exercises that follow can be used as and when it seems right and possible for you.

Important events in your life

You may remember that in Chapter 3 I made a list of important events that seemed to have triggered eating disorders in my clients. This is a good place to start an investigation of what important event may have contributed to *your* problems. Here is an exercise which you can do to see what you can discover.

Think about when your eating disorders really began to be a problem to you. Lots of people with eating disorders can trace difficulties with food back a very long way, but there is often a time that can be more or less accurately pinpointed when it obviously became worse. For an anorexic, it will probably be the first significant weight loss, for a bulimic the beginning of a pattern of bingeing and vomiting, even though that may have been something you did occasionally before then.

When you have pinpointed that time, which may span several months, think about what else was happening in your life around that time or a little earlier. If nothing springs to mind immediately, think about the different areas of your life and what was happening to each of them:

- family
- relationships
- friends and social life
- school/college
- work

It is likely that you will be able to identify some major event in your life that caused you a lot of emotion (good or bad), and that in some way caused a significant change. If you can identify such an event, try and work on it by asking yourself these questions:

1 Does it make sense to me that I might have started to have an eating disorder as a reaction to that event?
2 What feelings were aroused in me by that event? In particular were there contradictory feelings, eg happiness/anxiety, anger/fear, pleasure/shame?

3 Was there anyone that I could share these feelings with at the time?
4 Could it be true that I was trying to deal with an event or situation without enough help? Would I now expect a child or young person to be able to cope with that situation at that age?

When you try to answer these questions and explore this crucial event or situation, you can think of using the support available to you in two ways. First, you can be helped to find out more. For instance, if there was some major event in your family, how were other people affected and how might that in turn have affected you? For example one young woman's father died very suddenly of a heart attack when she was 17. That was bad enough, but her mother was also severely affected by her husband's death and became depressed, so that she was unable to offer much support to her daughter. This is the kind of information that people who were adult at the time will be able to give you, even if you cannot remember yourself. Think about members of your family (especially those one step away, such as aunts, uncles and cousins), neighbours, teachers or family friends as potential sources of help. You may well be amazed at what other people can tell you, and at how they saw and understood that things were difficult for you.

Secondly, use your support to talk about this event as much as you possibly can. After all, it is likely that you will never have expressed to anybody the feelings that you had then, and that they are still locked inside you. Let yourself cry and be angry and sad and disappointed, or whatever the feelings are.

Really try to allow yourself to *share* these feelings with somebody. There will be a temptation to try and do it all on your own, but that is what you have already done and it was too much for you. This time, provide yourself with the sympathy and listening and understanding that you have not had before.

Expect to find more than one feeling. Expect to find opposite and contradictory feelings. It is often those contradictions that make it hard to express what we feel in the first place, especially if we are ashamed of some of the feelings. For instance, in the example I gave above, the girl whose father died was desperately sad that he died, but also in some part of her relieved because her father had been a very difficult, angry man. In yet another part of her she felt guilty because she had been a difficult, angry teenager and she and her father had had lots of arguments; she wondered if all that stress and tension had contributed to his death. This combination of feelings was not easy to admit to, but is really quite understandable. When they had been expressed to someone else, they did not feel nearly so dreadful and shameful.

Really work as hard as you can to extract the feelings from this event. Use whatever you can think of to bring yourself close to them: photographs, diaries, other people's recollections. Draw it, paint it, act it, dance it, write about it. Give it the importance and attention it never received from you or anybody else before. It must have been important if you needed your eating disorder to cope with it. Think of what you are doing now as a better way of dealing with the difficult events and situations that we all meet in life.

Do not expect to find this a particularly easy or enjoyable process. If it were, you would have done it long since. Think of it as necessary emotional work; think of it as lessons in allowing yourself to know what you feel. Bring to it all the energy, determination and perseverance that you used in maintaining your eating disorder. You can expect to learn a lot about yourself just from doing this one thing, and probably feel considerable relief from dealing actively and directly with something that was very important to you.

Your life

This next exercise is designed to help you see how your life has been, to let you tell your story. You may not have been able to identify one specific event or circumstance which triggered your eating disorder, in which case this exercise may help you see what accumulated stresses you have had to deal with, and why you have needed to mis-use food to enable you to cope. You may think you already know the story of your life, but I think you will find in terms of your emotional history – how things affected you, how you felt – you have not really let your-self know how it has been for you.

Again this is not an exercise that you are likely to find great fun because it will bring up all sorts of difficult feel-ings and memories. Again you must do it when it feels right for you. An exercise like this can take months. Again, use your support to talk through it all as thoroughly as you can. Your goal is to find the feelings and express them. For that you need a listener and a companion so that you do not simply feel the trauma all over again on your own.

The task is to create your autobiography, using your memories and the help of whoever and whatever else is available to you. There are all sorts of ways of doing this and you must choose or invent the one that suits you and your talents best. The following is a list of ways in which I have seen people do this exercise. You may want to use one of them, or bits of different ones, or find your own way of doing it.

1 **A diary.** You can write your autobiography by making chapters for different ages and describing what hap-pened at that time. Remember, the point of it is to find the feelings involved in what happened, so that you can consider discussing each bit in turn with your support and using that opportunity to express the feelings. So we are not just talking about your baby brother being

born, or moving house, but how you *felt* about those events. That is what you have had to hide, even from yourself, and it is most important you do not do the same thing again. Photographs can make good illustrations for this diary, or you can draw or paint your own. This way of creating your autobiography often suits people who like writing and who enjoy the feeling of creating a volume of their own.

2 **A life line.** Another way to provide a written account is by plotting the story of your life along a line which is marked with your age. This takes the form of notes, and it can also be illustrated with words or colours to show feelings. So a little section might look something like this:

Upper Sixth year.
Liked French and English,
Hated history (Mr Brown ugh!)

Went out with Roger – 6 months	Applying to universities
Horrible break-up.	Wanted/didn't want to
Parents having money probs.	leave home.

17————————————   18————————

angry	anxious	scared
depressed	scared	excited
	annoyed	anxious

interested, bored, anxious, pleased

You will need more time with your supporter with this form, so that you can explain what your notes mean and describe in more detail what was going on for you as well as how you felt.

3 **Drawing and painting.** If you like using colours and shapes (even if you are not good at technical painting or drawing) this can be a good way to represent both events and feelings. It can take the form of a series of 'snapshots', or it can be more like a woven piece of fabric with different strands or patterns. You can include words if you like, or photographs or whatever else seems useful.

Here you will need quite a lot of time with your helper to share and explore what you have done, and to 'translate' the language of painting into words. This is not primarily for the helper's benefit, but for yours. You need the experience of sharing your life and feelings with someone else, to discover that you do not have to manage them all on your own.

4 **Music and/or dance.** If you are particularly interested and involved in these ways of expressing yourself, they also can be used as a way of sharing your history. Think of the music and dance as a bridge from the feelings that you have never shared to the words with which you can allow someone to know you, and thus come to know yourself better.

However you do it – and you may well be able to find your own particular way – the point is to come to a greater awareness of your own emotional history and to share and develop that awareness with your supporter. It will very likely become very much clearer to you what you have needed your eating disorder for.

Your family

In considering your own emotional history and your own life you will inevitably have had to think about your family and how it has operated. In this section I make some suggestions about how you can think further about the workings of your family and how they have affected you.

1 The first and most obvious way is to share with your family what you have been doing to create your autobiography. In an ideal situation it would be possible to share everything with everyone, but that is unlikely. Instead you will have to choose the bits that seem easiest to share first, and who is likely to be able or willing to hear what you have to say and tell you in their turn

how things were for them. You may well come from a family where this is not the usual way of going on, so it is likely to feel strange and dangerous, but you may be surprised at how much response you get.

2 Turn back to Chapter 3 and look at how the dynamic in Elaine's family was described by thinking about who was allowed to have which feelings. See if you can work out an equivalent scheme for your family. You can also do this by naming the roles that were played by the various members of the family, eg victim, strong person, delinquent, ill person, helpless one, director general and so on, remembering that people often play several roles.

This whole area is discussed in Skynner and Cleese, *Families and How to Survive Them* (details in Further Reading). Sometimes families are brave enough to try and read this book together as a way of discussing what went on in their family. It is in this sort of a way that your illness can become an opportunity for growth for all of you rather than just a disaster for you.

In relation to yourself and your eating disorder, however, you are trying to understand specifically why in your family situation you had to develop an eating disorder to deal with your feelings. How was it, you want to know, that your feelings could not be expressed in more obvious and open ways? Check your ideas with your supporter.

Your relationship with food

A further area for exploration is why, for you particularly, food has gained such enormous emotional power and significance. This can also relate to history. Try the following exercise as a way of getting in touch with what food has meant to you as you have been growing up.

Think about how food was used in your family and ask yourself the following questions:

1 How much money, time and effort went into food and its preparation? Was there tension and difficulty in these areas?
2 Who did most of the food preparation? What feelings did that person have about it?
3 What were meal times like? Were they occasions of pleasure, relaxation, enjoyment, tension, argument, aggression?
4 How was the family dynamic demonstrated at meal times? Did people play their usual roles?
5 Was food used as a threat, weapon or punishment? Was it used as a comfort, bribe or reward?
6 Were there rules about access to food between meals? Whose rules were they? Did they make sense in the family circumstances? Were they used for other emotional purposes.

Try sharing and comparing the results of all these questions with your supporter. We all think the way our family did these things is the only way they can be done, and it can be quite surprising to discover the range of possibilities.

Spend some time considering how this way of using food in your family affects you now. You may be surprised to find that you are repeating patterns and attitudes you learned then. You are looking for the roots of your present attitudes to food.

Your relationship with your body

We have no existence apart from our bodies; there is no 'me' that can be detached from my body. Research suggests in fact that as children our sense of ourselves *is* our sense of our body. It is then very interesting and important to consider how you came to your present sense of displeasure and non-acceptance of your body. Where did you learn that? Ask yourself the following questions as a way into thinking about this issue.

1 What do you think your mother/family's attitudes to your body might have been at the following ages:

- 0–5
- 5–10
- 11–15

What do you think you learned about yourself and your body as a result?

2 How did you find out about puberty and menstruation? What were the feelings around that?

3 When do you think you were first consciously aware of your body and how you look? What are the feelings around that first memory?

4 How have you felt about the way you look in relation to your peer group?

5 How important do you think the cultural demand for you to be thin has been? When did you become aware of it?

Having an eating disorder involves hating and attacking your body; getting rid of one involves learning not to do that and instead accepting and taking care of your body. If you can sort out where all the hating came from, you will have more freedom to choose whether you want to continue like that. Use your supporter to discuss these things and also to compare somebody else's experience with your own.

CHAPTER 6

Professional Help

In the last chapter I gave some idea of how someone with an eating disorder can start to work on recovering. How do you know when this is possible and when it would be better to look for professional help?

1 The first criterion, and the most important, is what you, the sufferer, feel you can manage and what you want. If, when you read the last chapter, you felt energized, enthused and optimistic, then you have the best possible basis for working on yourself. If, however you felt that it was too difficult and you did not have the energy to try and that it just made you feel depressed and hopeless, then maybe you should look for some professional help.
2 The second issue to consider carefully is how much support you can find if you are going to try on your own. The underlying difficulty for you has been that you have not had enough support in the past. It is important that you do not just repeat the original trauma by trying to deal with everything on your own all over again. You will have realized from reading the last chapter that you need people who can give you the time and space to go through a process of recovery. Those people need to understand what you are asking of them, and must be strong enough to stand your pain and difficulty. If you cannot find people like that, then you probably need a professional helper.
3 If you have been ill a long time, and are physically

unwell or at risk, and/or if your patterns of food misuse and anorexic/bulimic thinking are deeply ingrained, then you need professional help. In this situation you may well not be able to ask for help yourself and somebody else, usually your family, will find it for you.

4 If you have other problems, either physical such as diabetes or pregnancy, or psychological such as drug or alcohol addiction, then you need professional help.

What professional help can offer you

Professional help sometimes is talked about as if it were some kind of miraculous intervention that will magically and painlessly cure the sufferer. I suppose that is what we all secretly long for: painless recovery. However, there are no miracles and the process of recovery has to be worked and suffered through by you and those close to you, whether or not you have professional help. The price of recovery is to face the pain.

However, what good professional help can offer is a firmer setting and stronger support than the average person can establish for themselves. It will provide help along something like the following lines.

MANAGEMENT OF THE EATING BEHAVIOUR

Whether you are an inpatient or a regular outpatient, and depending on how ill you are, somebody else will be weighing you or asking how much you weigh, taking an active part in helping you to change your eating patterns. Especially at the beginning, and if your weight is dangerously low, this can often be a great relief – somebody else is taking at least part of the responsibility for ensuring that you are properly nourished. The task of taking care of yourself, of attending to your needs all alone has proved too much for you and now somebody else will help. This aspect of inpatient care is often also a huge relief to families who are at their wits' end and frightened by the sufferer's condition.

Of course it is not that simple. As I have explained, your eating disorder has been your way of coping, you have needed it, and while you still feel you need it you will not be willing to give it up. The best professional help will recognize the importance of your eating disorder to you. A professional of this kind will not simply force on you a refeeding programme of a huge number of calories, but will try and find and collaborate with that part of you that wants to recover and knows that you need to change the way you use food. But the more ill you are, both physically and psychologically, the less you are likely to be able to find that healthy, nurturing part of you. As a result the professional helpers will take a proportionately greater share of the responsibility for nourishing you.

At its most extreme, for anorexics and bulimarexics, this will mean being fed through a needle in a vein. The next most extreme measure involves being fed through a tube which goes up your nose and down the back of your throat into your stomach. But neither of these can possibly be long-term solutions; they are emergency measures. They will be succeeded by a combination of a liquid diet and some real food, and then by a diet which is generally around 3,000 calories a day. This will result in you gaining weight at the rate of approximately 2lbs (1kg) a week. Some clinicians now think this is too fast and will proceed on the basis of you gaining about ½–1lb (225–450g) a week.

Because your eating disorder has been necessary to you, all this will be extremely frightening. Even if you are not at a low weight, but are seriously bulimic, the regime of regular and controlled meals is still likely to be horrifying.

In these circumstances, whether you are anorexic or bulimic, it is very easy indeed for you to forget altogether the part of you that wants to live, wants to recover, wants to be well. It is very easy to turn into a 100 per cent anorexic or bulimic who sees the help being offered as an attempt to destroy what is most precious and necessary for you. If it seems like this to you, then you will of course resist.

It is this resistance and how it is managed that is the single most difficult aspect of the physical recovery programme, and is the source of a great many horror stories about inpatient treatment. At its worst doctor and patient get locked into an angry and destructive battle which ends with the patient discharging herself or the doctor throwing her out. It is extremely hard for you to keep finding the part of you that wants help, and just as hard for your professional helpers to keep reminding themselves that you are very scared and very angry, and that they must be very patient.

In the long run you must find the part of you that recognizes the need to eat normally, because nobody else can do that for you. The tragic deaths of anorexics and bulimics occur when it has just not been possible for the sufferer or anyone else to mobilize that healthy part.

There are two methods of trying to overcome your resistance to eating normally in an inpatient setting, both of which are becoming less common as clinicians work harder at finding the healthy and responsible bit of you. The first of these is to watch you closely to make sure that you do not destroy the food you are supposed to be eating, or continue with a pattern of vomiting or laxative abuse. This usually means a helper staying with you while you eat and for at least an hour afterwards, including accompanying you to the bathroom. The second method is to institute a reward system for doing what you are supposed to do: gain weight and/or stop vomiting or purging. This is sometimes referred to as a token economy system. Usually it means that your life in hospital is organized round winning privileges such as being allowed to get out of bed to go to the bathroom, getting dressed, leaving the ward, making phone calls, etc.

If you are being treated as an outpatient, the assumption

will have been made, after discussion with you, that it is possible for you (and often your family) to find a way of managing your resistance to recovery without actually admitting you to hospital. Sometimes people with eating disorders are treated as day patients of a unit in order to provide a halfway house to responsibility. Sometimes your family will be asked to collaborate, for instance by providing specified meals at specified times for you. The more confidence the professionals have in your capacity to use the part of you that wants to get well, the more responsibility they will give you for managing your own resistance. So for example, at the healthiest end of the continuum, you will probably be asked to collaborate in devising a mealplan for yourself, given some guidelines about dealing with problems and then given regular appointments to monitor how you are managing.

COGNITIVE APPROACHES TO YOUR EATING DISORDER

The second ingredient in any professional approach to an eating disorder is the exploration and discussion of your ideas about food, weight, shape, and size. The idea is to show you, at a commonsense, rational level, that your ideas on these matters are mistaken. This is likely to cover the same areas that were mentioned in this context in Chapter 5: eating behaviour, body image and self-esteem.

PSYCHOTHERAPEUTIC APPROACHES TO YOUR EATING DISORDER

In addition to these two elements of behavioural and cognitive therapy, the best programmes of recovery will include the whole area of your emotional history, the expression of feelings and your development as a person. Many professionals now think that these three elements go hand in hand and should match each other, so for example a weight gain programme should be slow and in stages, to allow you to develop alternative ways of being as you go along.

In a hospital setting this three-part approach will be dealt with by different people, but the less ill you are the more likely they are to be three elements of a recovery programme co-ordinated by one helper. A psychotherapist in private practice, for example, who specializes in eating disorders, will include these different elements in the therapy.

Some psychotherapists do not pay any attention to behavioural or cognitive approaches at all. However, these therapies do not have a good success rate, so you should ask about this in any initial assessment or interview. You need the realities of your eating behaviour and the compulsive/obsessive aspects to be taken very seriously, unless you are already well on the road to recovery and managing these aspects well yourself.

Some cognitive therapists do not think that a psychotherapeutic element is necessary in a recovery programme. Cognitive therapy, for example, has very good rates of success with bulimia. I can understand that cognitive therapy can change attitudes to food, weight, shape and size. It is harder for me to see how it addresses the development of the person.

The issues that psychotherapy addresses are the same areas that were discussed in Chapters 3 and 4 and in the section of knowing yourself better in Chapter 5: the relationship you have with your own history, your family and your life. Professional help will try and get you to contact the feelings you have about these issues.

The therapeutic relationship

Psychotherapy is based on the conviction that we need a relationship with someone in order to be able to face the difficult emotional issues in our lives. If, for whatever reason, our families have not fulfilled or cannot fulfil that role well enough, then we will need additional help. People often find that help among those around them. In the last chapter I stressed the need for support in order for you to have the strength and courage to look at all the things that trouble you. A therapist's job is to be that person when there is no one in your life to take that role: to listen, to accept, to understand, to help you see who you are, sometimes to challenge.

In a good therapeutic relationship you will come to trust and rely on the therapist so that you can feel safe enough to be more open about yourself than you have ever been. If you have had an eating disorder for years there will be all sorts of things that you need to process and deal with. Many therapists now think that an eating disorder puts emotional development on hold, so that as you recover you will have some catching up to do.

I do not believe that these processes can possibly take place in a few weeks. It makes no sense to me that a person can have an eating disorder from the age of 15 to 20, and recover from it in six months. I think that the eating behaviour can sometimes change that quickly, which is often an enormous relief, especially for bulimics, but you need more time for deeper changes. Have these thoughts in mind when you look for help.

You should also remember that any therapy is only as good as the relationship with the therapist. When you are being assessed by a therapist, remember that you are also assessing that person, and in particular making a judgement about whether you can at least begin to share with him or her the things that trouble you.

FAMILY THERAPY

Because so many people with eating disorders are young and still living with or deeply involved with their families, many recovery programmes will offer family therapy which will try and explore what has been going on in your family so that you have needed an eating disorder.

It takes an enormous amount of courage for a family to allow an outsider to look at what goes on inside it, but potentially I think the changing of family dynamics and relationships is the most creative possible outcome of an eating disorder. After all, if the sufferer recovers then one person's pain has been resolved; if a whole family gets well then huge potential for good for a lot more people is generated.

ARTS THERAPIES

I have stressed throughout this book, the core problem in both anorexia and bulimia is a difficulty in being aware of and expressing feelings. Many therapists now think that non-verbal expressions of feelings are helpful in developing a bridge towards an ability to express them more freely and in words. Arts, drama, music and dance are now often included in professional recovery programmes. For an anorexic or bulimic who is very unused to naming or identifying feelings, these other modes of expression can be very helpful.

SETTING OUT ON THE ROAD TO RECOVERY

If you decide that you want to try and recover, with or without professional help, you will need all the strength and courage you possess. On the other hand, you are likely to emerge from the process a stronger person with a better sense of self. You will have learned a lot about yourself, developed a greater capacity to take responsibility for yourself, grown as a human being. The process of recovery can also provide the opportunity for you to set out on the long path of becoming who you could be; becoming yourself and developing your potential in a way that few of us do. None of us undertakes deep change just because it seems like a nice idea; we change because we cannot stand the way we are any longer. If the pain of your eating disorder is goading you towards change, you are undoubtedly suffering. That distress can also provide you with the energy you need to take hold of your life with both hands.

Further Reading

The following books are suggested for additional reading.

Bruch, Hilde, *The Golden Cage: The Enigma of Anorexia Nervosa*, Open Books Publishing, 1978
Although this is not a new book it is very interesting because Bruch was the first person to describe anorexia as developing within a family system that could not allow feelings to be expressed. The system she describes is the prosperous middle-class family that controls every aspect of a girl's life, so that her anorexia constitutes the only possible way of escaping.

Buckroyd, Julia, *Eating Your Heart Out*, 2nd edition, Optima, 1994
In this book I describe a range of the emotional meanings that eating disorders might have and the kinds of personal traumas and social pressures that trigger them. The last part of the book provides ideas about how a person with an eating disorder might set about working on her emotional development.

Cooper, Peter J, *Bulimia Nervosa: A Guide to Recovery*, Robinson Publishing, 1993
This is a valuable tool for bulimics looking for behavioural and cognitive approaches to resuming normal eating and putting an end to bingeing and vomiting. Two thirds of the book is a self-help manual for returning to normal food use.

Dana, Mira and Marilyn Lawrence, *Women's Secret Disorder: A New Understanding of Bulimia*, Grafton Books, 1988
This is a particularly useful book for understanding the personal and cultural meanings of bulimia. The authors are especially interested in the split in the bulimic woman between 'good' and 'bad' and how that split can be mended so that the woman can become more accepting of herself and more integrated. They are interested in why women suffer from eating disorders more than men and explore the idea that women are asked to perform more in the world than they ever have done, but at the same time are lacking the kind of confidence and self-esteem that would enable them to achieve their potential with less distress. The authors see eating disorders as an attempt to cope with the strain that this situation creates. There is also a chapter giving advice on how to set up a self-help group.

Dolan, Bridget and Inez Gitzinger, *Why Women: Gender Issues and Eating Disorders*, Athlone Press, 1994
'Anorexia nervosa and bulimia are the only psychological disorders which are specific to Western culture and the only ones so specific to woman.' This book is concerned with the debate about why that might be so and what it means. The subject is dealt with from a number of perspectives, including the individual and family background and the relevance of socio-cultural issues. It is a fairly academic book and not aimed at the general reader, but nevertheless important and interesting as a contribution to the debate.

Dryden, Wendy and Colin Feltham, *Counselling and Psychotherapy: A Consumer's Guide*, Sheldon Press, London, 1995
This book describes the range of available therapies in Britain, and should enable you to decide which one might be right for you.

Duker, Marilyn and Roger Slade, *Anorexia Nervosa and Bulimia: How to Help*, Oxford University Press, 1988
An excellent but rather technical book, directed towards

professionals. However, it covers many of the same issues as this book in more detail. Good further reading, especially for helpers.

Eichenbaum, Luise and Susie Orbach, *Understanding Women*, Penguin 1983
This book discusses how women come to have the psychological uncertainties and insecurities that are so common among us. The authors focus on how girls are brought up within the family, especially the relationship between mother and daughter, and describe how the mother's own experience of not having her emotional needs met creates a pattern that repeats in the next generation with her daughter.

Hay, Louise, *You Can Heal Your Life*, Eden Grove Editions, 1988
A classic from the self-help literature. Very enthusiastic but well worth reading.

Maine, Margo, *Father Hunger*, Simon & Schuster, 1993
This book focuses on the relationship between fathers and adolescent daughters as one of the roots of eating disorders. The author describes the way in which male needs for separatedness and self-reliance are at odds with female needs for connectedness and relationship. The adolescent girl longs for closeness and acceptance from her father; his failure to meet this need leads to 'father hunger' and to eating disorders as a way of coping with it. The author makes suggestions as to how fathers can improve their relationships with their daughters.

Norwood, Robyn, *Women Who Love Too Much*, Arrow Books, 1986
A book which tries to explain why women can find themselves involved in a series of abusive and unsatisfying relationships with men. The author locates the roots of the

problem in the woman's experience within her own family and discusses how the pattern can be changed.

Orbach, Susie, *Fat is a Feminist Issue*, Arrow Books, 1988
Strictly speaking this is a book about compulsive eating rather than anorexia or bulimia, but the author is extremely interesting both on the cultural processes that makes women obsessive about being 'thin' and also on the meanings of food misuse for the individual. Although it was first published in 1978, it has definitely stood the test of time.

Orbach, Susie, *Fat is a Feminist Issue II*, Arrow Books, 1984
A self-help manual packed with useful information and ideas, and with a lot of information on forming self-help groups.

Orbach, Susie, *Hunger Strike: The Anorexic's Struggle as a Metaphor for our Age*, Penguin, 1993
The first part of this book is a remarkable and sophisticated account of the inner world of the anorexic. Its compassion and understanding make it an extremely valuable resource. The second part discusses what kind of help can enable the anorexic to accept her needs and feelings and make the emotional growth which will render the anorexia unnecessary. Not a particularly easy read, but well worth the effort.

Skynner, Robin and John Cleese, *Families and How to Survive Them*, Mandarin, 1993
An excellent introduction to the importance of our families in determining our attitudes and assumptions. A book which provides the tools for understanding your own family and its dynamics. The book is written in a dialogue form and puts over a great many key ideas in a very accessible way.

Welbourne, Jill and Joan Purgold, *The Eating Sickness:*

Anorexia, Bulimia and the Myth of Suicide by Slimming, Harvester Press, 1984
A book about anorexia and bulimarexia which is particularly good on the anorexic's world view. The authors discuss at length the need for collaboration and co-operation between doctors, family and anorexic, and describe in detail the way they believe weight gain should be paralleled by therapeutic progress.

West, Richard, *Eating Disorders: Anorexia and Bulimia Nervosa*, Office of Health Economics, 12, Whitehall, London SW1A 2DY, 1994
This pamphlet gives a brief overview of anorexia and bulimia and gathers together the most recent research on who suffers from these conditions, why and what treatments are available. Although it is rather factual and impersonal, it also includes some illustrative case histories and provides an excellent introduction to the subject.

Woolf, Naomi, *The Beauty Myth*, Vintage, 1991
A very trenchant piece of writing which sees the cultural demand for thinness as just the latest way in which women are kept in their places, and indeed keep themselves there.

Useful Addresses

AUSTRALIA

The Anorexia and Bulimia Nervosa Foundation
1513 High Street
Glen Iris
3156 Victoria
Tel: 613 885 0318

CANADA

Bulimia Anorexia Nervosa Association
c/o Psychological Service
University of Windsor
Ontario N9B 3PH
Tel: 519 253 7421, 519 253 7545

National Eating Disorder Information Center
College Wing Room 211, 1st Floor
200 Elizabeth Street
Toronto
Ontario N5G 2C4
Tel: 416 340 4156

NEW ZEALAND

Women with Eating Disorders Resource Centre
PO Box 4520
Armagh and Montreal Streets
Christchurch
Tel: 643 366 7725

SOUTH AFRICA

Dr D LeGrange
Dept of Psychology
University of Cape Town
Rondebosch 7700
Cape Town
Tel: 021 650 9111

UK

British Association of Counselling
1 Regent Place
Rugby
CV21 3BJ
Tel: 01788 578328
Publishes a Directory of Counsellors which should be available in most libraries. Otherwise you can get them to send you the entries for your area. The directory lists both organizations and individuals. If you are looking for low-cost or free counselling you may well be able to get it via one of the listed organizations. You should note, however, that inclusion of individuals in the BAC Directory does not imply any kind of vetting except for those counsellors marked 'accredited'.

Eating Disorders Association
Sackville Place
Magdalen St
Norwich
NR3 1JU
Helpline: 01603 621414
Youth Helpline: 01603 765050
Recorded Message: 0891 615466
This charity is an indispensable aid to finding information about help for anorexia and bulimia in the UK. It co-ordinates and distributes information about academic research via its journal, *The European Journal of Eating Disorders*, but is also a support organization for sufferers and distributes a magazine, *Signpost*, to members. It also runs conferences and co-ordinates a network of self-help groups and telephone supporters.

Institute for Family Therapy
43 New Cavendish Street
London W1M 7RB
Tel: 0171 935 1651
NHS family therapy can sometimes be arranged via social services with a GP referral.

United Kingdom Council for Psychotherapy
Regents College
Inner Circle
Regents Park
London NW1 4NS
The umbrella organization for therapists in Britain. They have usually had longer and more thorough training than counsellors. The membership is grouped according to theoretical orientation, so that if you have looked at the Dryden book (see Further Reading) you will be able to choose someone from the background you feel most drawn to.

The Women's Therapy Centre
6 Manor Gardens
London N7 6SZ
Tel: 0171 263 6200
A pioneer in low-cost therapy for eating disorders.

USA

Adolescent Anorexia Treatment Program
Children's Hospital of Michigan
3901 Beaubien Boulevard
Detroit
Michigan 48201
Tel: 313 745 4878

National Eating Disorders Association
Lauriate Psychiatric Clinic and Hospital
6655 South Yale Avenue
Tulsa
Oklahoma 74136
Tel: 918 481 4092

Residential In-Patient Program for Eating Disorders
The Renfew Center
7700 Renfrew Lane
Coconut Creek
Florida 33073
Tel: 305 698 9222

and

The Renfrew Center
475 Spring Lane
Philadelphia
Pennsylvania 19128
Tel: 215 482 5353

Index

ELEMENT BOOKS LTD
PUBLISHERS

Element is an independent general publishing house. Our list includes titles on Religion, Personal Development, Health, Native Traditions, Modern Thought and Current Affairs, and is probably the most comprehensive collection of books in its sphere.

To order direct from Element Books, or to join the Element Club without obligation and receive regular details of great offers, please contact:
Customer Services, Element Books Ltd, Longmead, Shaftesbury, Dorset SP7 8PL, England.   Tel: 01747 851339   Fax: 01747 851394

Or you can order direct from your nearest distributor:

UK and Ireland
Penguin Group Distribution Ltd,
Bath Road, Harmondsworth,
Middlesex UB7 0DA, England.
Tel: 0181 899 4000
Fax: 0181 899 4020/4030

Canada
Penguin Books Canada Ltd,
10 Alcorn Avenue, Suite 300,
Toronto, Ontario MV4 3B2.
Tel: (416) 925 2249
Fax: (416) 925 0068

Central & South America & the Caribbean
Humphrey Roberts Associates,
24 High Street,
London E11 2AQ, England.
Tel: 0181 530 5028
Fax: 0181 530 7870

USA
Viking Penguin Inc,
375 Hudson Street, New York,
NY 10014.
Tel: (212) 366 2000
Fax: (212) 366 2940

Australia
Jacaranda Wiley Ltd, PO Box
1226, Milton, Queensland 4064.
Tel: (7) 369 9755 Fax: (7) 369 9155

New Zealand
Forrester Books NZ Ltd,
3/3 Marken Place, Glenfield,
Auckland 10.
Tel: 444 1948   Fax: 444 8199

Other areas:
Penguin Paperback Export Sales,
27 Wrights Lane,
London W8 5TZ, England.
Tel: 0171 416 3000
Fax: 0171 416 3060

The Health Essentials Series

Comprehensive, high-quality introductions to complementary healthcare

Each book in the *Health Essentials* series is written by a practising expert in their field, and presents all the essential information on each therapy, explaining what it is and how it works. Advice is also given, where possible, on how to begin using the therapy at home, together with comprehensive lists of courses and classes available worldwide.

In this series:

128/144 pages • 216 x 138 mm • Paperback • Line illustrations
UK £5.99 • USA $9.95 • Canada $12.99

The Natural Way Series

**Comprehensive guides to gentle, safe and effective treatments
for today's common illnesses**

Element's innovative *Natural Way* series provides practical and authoritative information on holistic and orthodox treatments for our most common illnesses. Endorsed by both the British Holistic Medical Association and the American Holistic Medical Association, these concise guides explain clearly what the disease is, how and why it occurs, and what can be done about it. Each book includes advice on helping yourself and where to turn to for outside qualified help.

In this series:

128/144 pages • 178 x 111 mm • Paperback • Line illustrations
UK £3.99 • USA $5.95 • Canada $7.99